Sufficient Grace when Your Life is in the Sewer

Life is not fair, but God is good

Pastor Rodney Bankens

Copyright © 2008 by Pastor Rodney Bankens

Sufficient Grace when Your Life is in the Sewer
by Pastor Rodney Bankens

Printed in the United States of America

ISBN 978-1-60477-734-5

All rights reserved solely by the author. The author guarantees all contents are original and do not infringe upon the legal rights of any other person or work. No part of this book may be reproduced in any form without the permission of the author. The views expressed in this book are not necessarily those of the publisher.

Unless otherwise indicated, Bible quotations are taken from the King James Version and from the Holy Bible, New Living Translation®. Copyright © 1996, 2004 by Tyndale Charitable Trust. The Scriptures are in italics per the writer of this manuscript.

www.xulonpress.com

Dedicated

To my wonderful wife of forty years, for being there and standing with me through all the ups and downs of life. Sandy is a great Christian and a lady who walks by faith and trusts God in every venue of life.s

To my two son's, Robbie and Kevin, who have added so much to my life and I love them so much. Many of my stories include them, because they have been my life.

To my wonderful, godly parents, Johnnie, Jr. and Barbara Bankens, who raised me in the ways of God. Their lives have been great examples for me to follow.

To Dr. M. D. Treece and Sister Betty Treece. My pastor and his beautiful wife. These folks are the reason for my being what I am today. These wonderful people salvaged me and my family after others had given up hope. The greatest pastor and wife. These are holy and godly people that I love with all my heart.

To Rev. Rick Treece and Sister Diane Treece. A great young couple that have taken over the helm of my home church. They are doing a marvelous job of keeping the vision of Dr. M. D. Treece alive, while bringing Apostolic Temple to new heights in the work of God.

To Apostolic Temple and all the great saints of God there. Thanks for loving me in spite of my faults and failures. Thanks for being there when I was in need.

My life is so much better today because of all the people that have touched me.

Preface

This manuscript has been in the making for several years. It is a compilation of several of the messages that I have preached while I evangelized. This book will share with you many of the life changing stories that have changed my life and continue to affect my life today. I do not consider myself to be a writer by any means. It is with much reservation that I have even taken this to a publisher and set it into a book form. I do it not for its perfection of grammar, punctuation, or spelling, but because it's content may change a life.

If you could only see how I prepared my sermon notes in the beginning of my ministry and how I prepare them today. Quickly you would understand I have not had anyone teach me how this is done. I have set my notes up from the very beginning of my ministry, to be user friendly. If someone else would by chance ever get my notes to speak or preach from they could use them.

I have taken these prepared notes as my reference point to write this book. What I am actually doing is preaching my sermons through this media called a book. I hope that somewhere in this manuscript will be the words that will change someone's life. I hope that it will have an effect on everyone that takes time to read from these pages.

I was a forty year old man, with many problems in my own personal life when I surrendered to the Lord to preach. I hope the contents of this manuscript will help someone who is in a time of decision in their own life.

Please do not spend all your time looking over the errors of my writing, read the content.

I wish that I could give credit to everyone that has had any input in my ministry. I have read many books, pamphlets, magazines during my lifetime. I have listened to my pastors preach, other preachers preach. I have listened to tapes, CD's and watched many Video's and DVD's. Yes, and by the way I do read and study the Bible. I do not know where every phrase in these chapters has been gleaned, but they are by no means my own and most are not even original. But, I will say the stories are mine and the format is mine and I have preached some of these messages over one hundred times in the past twenty years. I have no problem with you preaching from my book and even you calling it your own as long as you are pointing souls to Jesus Christ and His saving Grace.

In His Service,
Rodney Bankens

II Corinthians 12:6-10 KJV,
"For though I would desire to glory, I shall not be a fool; for I will say the truth; for now I forebear, lest any man should think of me above that which he seeth me to be, or he heareth of me.
And lest I should be exalted above measure through the abundance of the revelations, there was given to me a thorn in the flesh, the messenger of Satan to buffet me, lest I should be exalted above measure.
For this thing I besought the Lord thrice, that it might depart from me.
And he said unto me, my grace is sufficient for thee: for my strength is made perfect in weakness, most gladly therefore will I glory in my infirmities, that the power of Christ may rest upon me.
Therefore I take pleasure in infirmities, in reproaches, in necessities, in persecutions, in distresses for Christ sake: for when I am weak then am I strong."

CHAPTER ONE

"Sufficient Grace, when Your Life is in The Sewer!"

This subject of sufficient grace is a very simple subject; yet it is something we all need to hide deep within our hearts. It is something we all need to understand. When sickness comes, sorrows come, temptations come, troubles come, and even when death comes. If we are full of the Holy Spirit we have Grace sufficient for the hour.

We have all heard grace preached about many different times. I have preached about grace on many different occasions and in many different settings. Actually, when I first started preaching I said that I would never preach on the subject of grace; because grace is such a misused term in the Christian religious circles today. Today the majority of Christian groups preach a watered down grace. They preach that all you need to do is accept Christ as your personal Savior, His grace then covers you and you are forever saved. They preach no conversion experience, or new birth experience is necessary to receive God's Grace. Basically, they lead us to believe, once you have His Grace you can live as you please, even sin, because grace covers all of that. The formula they are preaching today is:

"Grace + nothing (0) = Salvation."

But I contend, that "Grace + nothing = Grace." It takes "God's Grace + your faith + obedience to the Word of God = Salvation."

Let's see what sufficient grace is: **Sufficient** (Webster) - *enough; as much as is needed.*

Grace (Strong's) - *The divine influence upon a heart and the reflection that portrays from that life.* Sufficient Grace simply means: You have enough influence from God; that no matter where you are; in sickness, troubles, trials, temptations, even if it is death; you will reflect Jesus Christ through your words, deeds and actions.

In this text, we see the Apostle Paul had a thorn in the flesh. (*I am not going to try to identify what I think the thorn was.*) But we do understand that whatever the thorn was, it hurt him, hindered him and vexed him. The bible says that Paul went to the Lord three times about the thorn. The literal translation indicates: "***three times he begged or pleaded with God to remove this thorn***." Can you imagine how Paul might have prayed? What he might have said to the Lord? I honestly believe Paul prayed like we pray over our situations. Maybe like this:

> *"Oh God, this thorn hurts me so"*
> *"Oh God, this thorn is hindering me*
> *From doing your will"*
> *"Oh God, this thorn is vexing me so"*

I do not know when the answer came, but somewhere in his prayer he received his answer from God. To his surprise his answer was ***"No Paul, I am** not going to remove the thorn, you are going to have to live with it."*

Most of us today cannot comprehend or even imagine, God telling this great Apostle, No. Why, the Apostle Paul is our hero of faith and was in the middle of God's perfect will. He was doing a great work for the Lord.

He was a faithful servant. He preached truth. He was an apostle, evangelist, missionary, preacher, teacher and a writer. He not only preached the Word, but he wrote over half of the New Testament scriptures in our bible. In the midst of Paul's praying, God said, *"No Paul, I am not going to remove the thorn; but my grace is sufficient for thee."*

You never read in the scriptures where Paul became offended at God. Nor do you see where Paul got upset. I honestly believe when Paul understood the answer; he stopped begging God and went to thanking and praising God. *"Alright Lord, if you are not going to remove the thorn, I'm going to thank you anyhow. I would rather keep this old thorn and have your grace than to lose the thorn and lose your grace also.*"

In the past twenty years, I have come in contact with many church members, saints of God, who seemingly were successful in their walk with God. You would see these people seemingly so strong at church; so strong in their praise and worship; so strong in all they are involved in at church. They would testify with such vigor and vitality, and then all of a sudden you notice they hardly praise and worship at all and they never testify anymore. They are no longer involved in anything at the church. Yes, they still attend, but that is all they do. If you do get a chance to talk with them you will notice they are so full of excuses, blaming all of their problems on someone else. They are placing the blame on the saints of the church, the pastor, their family, their spouse or even blaming God.

After much analyzing, I have found their problem is a lack of commitment. They can stay faithful, pray, praise, worship, testify and work for God as long as everything is good in their life. But you let them have the slightest problem; watch out, they are in big spiritual trouble.

The reason so many Christians live so defeated, is because the majority of them have never tested God's Grace. When we have a problem or a trial; when we get sick and are in pain; we bring this to the Lord. If God does not answer the way we feel he should, we begin to moan and complain. "Where is God when I need Him?" "Why, doesn't He hear me?" "God is just not listening to my needs." "Why doesn't God answer my prayers like He does all the other saints?" "See God just does not love me anymore."

Then we begin to have a pity party. This is exactly where Satan wants us; mixed up, confused, depressed, disoriented, and helpless. In this frame of mind we are now defenseless, helpless and of no threat to Satan.

Let me share the story of a young lady I met in a church a few years ago, (I will call her Janet). Janet was dating a young man, (I will call him Bill for the story sake). They were both talented with much music ability. Bill was a great musician and singer with aspirations of becoming a preacher. Janet had a great singing voice. During our first week of revival in this church, Bill jilted Janet and went back to his former girlfriend. Immediately they announced their plans for marriage, with the date of a wedding. Janet was devastated. I preached in that church four weeks. In the middle of the fourth week Janet came to the table my wife and I was sitting at in a restaurant and sat down. **Let me describe her demeanor to you:** Janet was already a petite young lady, but now she seemed to be wasting away to nothing. She was so heartbroken and sad. As she sat down at our table she said to me, "Brother, God is not answering my prayers. It's as though he does not care about my situation. I have prayed, I have fasted over three weeks and he does not seem to hear me." I spoke up and said, "Just a moment Sister Janet, God has heard your prayers; but you are not listening to His answer." She brightened up and a big smile came to her face and she so gently said to me, "Oh, what did God say that I did not hear?" I said, "He told you NO, you cannot marry the dude. Wipe your face, dry the tears from your eyes, and put a smile back on your face. God has a special beau, that will make you happy and together you two can fulfill the will of God." Janet did just that. Guess what? She is happily married to a fine young preacher and they are doing great in the will of God. Bill is also in the ministry, but He and his wife no longer preach the Acts 2 message of salvation. See what God spared Janet from. His Grace is so very sufficient.

As saints of God you need to understand that God does love you. He does hear your prayer. He does understand your sorrows, hurts, pains and agonies.

You must trust Him no matter what is happening. When you really learn to lean on Him, give Him your problems and lay all your burdens on Him; you will see through the eyes of faith He does hear you and He will answer your prayers. Why don't you just try God out ~ Give Him your petitions. Accept His answers and go ahead and give Him thanks. Praise Him and worship Him in spite of the trial, because His Grace is sufficient for you.

One of the number one gospel songs of all times is, "***Amazing Grace.***" This song is sung by folks of every creed and color all over this vast creation. It was written over two hundred years ago, by John Newton, a former slave trader.

> *"Amazing grace how sweet the sound,*
> *That saved a wretch like me!*
> *I once was lost, but now I am found,*
> *Was blind but now I see!"*

The great Apostle Paul of our text had not always been known as Paul, or as an Apostle. He was first known as Saul of Tarsus; a hot-headed, arrogant Pharisee. Saul knew the law of the Jews well and felt that anyone opposing his beliefs were worthy of death. Saul of Tarsus hated this new group who followed the teachings of Jesus Christ. He hated Christ and His teachings, calling it false. When he heard of such a group gathering, he angrily went after them. He would get letters from the High Priest and seek them out. He persecuted the people and played havoc with the church everywhere he went. He would have these people publicly beaten and often thrown in prison.

On his way to Damascus, with letters in his possession against those who were following the teachings of Christ Jesus; Saul of Tarsus was blinded by a bright light from heaven, and literally knocked to the ground. It was then that Saul heard the voice of the Lord speak directly to him;

Acts 9:4 (b) KJV
"...Saul, Saul, why persecutest thou me?"

Acts 9:5-8 KJV
"And he said, who art thou, Lord? And the
Lord said, I am Jesus, who thou persecutest.
It is hard for thee to kick against the pricks.
And he trembling and astonished said,
Lord what wilt thou have me to do?
And the Lord said unto him, arise, and go into the
city, and it shall be told thee what thou must do.

> *And the men who journeyed with him stood speechless, hearing a voice, but seeing no man. And Saul arose from the earth; and when his eyes were opened, he saw no man; but they led him by hand and brought him into Damascus."*

Saul of Tarsus was in the city three days without his sight. In those three days the Bible says he did not eat nor did he drink. The Lord was getting this man ready for a message. While Saul was being prepared to receive the message, God was preparing a preacher in that city with the message of truth for Saul of Tarsus. The Lord told Ananias of this venture. Ananias had some questions even some doubt about the situation. But the Lord assured him that Saul of Tarsus was a chosen vessel to carry this truth to the gentiles, kings and even the Jews who were scattered abroad.

I am sure, if we would have heard Saul of Tarsus talk to the Lord those three days; we would have heard much repenting. I can just imagine Saul admitting to the Lord, "I have been an awful man, even though at the time Lord, I thought I was doing your will I have been a sinner." "Lord, I have persecuted your followers, have had them publicly stripped, beaten and thrown in jail." "I have even stood by and watched some of them get stoned to death and did nothing for them." Lord, my sins are so great; they have been piling up from the moment of my birth." I honestly believe that somewhere in his repentance the Lord began to reveal to him,

"Yes, Saul you have sinned and fallen short of my glory; but my grace is sufficient even for you. My grace is greater than all of your sins." Somehow Saul of Tarsus understood what the Lord was revealing to him because he later wrote to the Romans these words;

Romans 5:20 KJV
"...but where sin abounded grace did much more abound."

When Ananias entered the house where Saul of Tarsus was; I honestly believe he found a man who had humbled himself and submitted himself to the will of God; a man who was repenting. Immediately Ananias laid his hand on Saul of Tarsus and began to speak, "Saul, this same Jesus who appeared unto you as you were coming to Damascus, is the same Jesus that has sent me to you. He wants to give your sight and also to fill you with the Holy Ghost." Immediately the scales fell from his eyes and he could see. He received the Holy Ghost, the Spirit of God within and was immediately taken to water and was baptized in the Name of Jesus Christ. Grace did not just cover Saul's sins; but the grace of God shined into his heart, then faith took action in his life as he obeyed the Word of God. Saul found salvation as did the one hundred twenty, including the twelve disciples and the mother of Jesus on the day of Pentecost. Saul was convicted of his sins and then began to repent. His sins were forgiven by Jesus Christ the supreme sacrificial lamb and the precious blood of Jesus Christ washed away Saul's sins. The grace of God began to shine forth from his ever changing life.

Ephesians 2:8 KJV
"For by grace are ye saved through faith, and that not of yourselves: it is the gift of God."

The same grace that changed Saul's life has changed many lives since and can change your life now. His grace is still sufficient today...for you.

GOD'S GRACE IS SUFFICIENT IN THE TIMES OF TRIALS AND SUFFERINGS:

The third verse of Amazing Grace:

*"Through many dangers toils and snares
I have already come, t'was grace that
Brought me safe thus far, and grace will
Lead me home."*

So many times after a person is filled with the Holy Ghost; after they know they have been changed; after they have been born again; they feel they should never have any more problems. Their life should be a life of wealth, health, and happiness from this moment until they get to heaven. Nowhere in the bible do I find that kind of guarantee. In fact, I find so much opposite.

Psalms 34:19 KJV, David said,
"Many are the afflictions of the righteous: but the Lord delivereth him out of them all."

Yes, even we saints of God, who have repented of our sins, who have been baptized in the Name of Jesus Christ and filled with His precious Holy Ghost will have many afflictions. We will face the problems of this life. We will face many trials. We will suffer, sicknesses, diseases and even suffer death; but His grace is sufficient through it all.

Writer's note:
"The word afflictions did not seem serious when I first read it in this scripture. It was something so simple: like a burr under a horse's blanket.

In the dictionary I found something quite amazing:

Afflictions~ *"Adversities, calamities, distresses, evils, harms, heaviness, troubles, wrongs, sorrows, hurts, etc, etc,"*

The good people who serve the Lord will not be exempt nor will they escape the troubles of this life. We will face life and these struggles just like everyone else. But, the Lord will be with those who love Him no matter what the situation. In fact, if you find your life in turmoil, God is there. If you are going through a fiery trial, God is in the fire with you. If you are sick or afflicted, God is with you. Wherever you as a child of God are, God is there. He walks beside you He guards and guides you in and through every situation of life. The Psalmist David, lets us all know, just because we are a child of God; this will not eliminate the hurts, pains, sufferings, sorrows, and heartaches of life. He does go on to say, that it does guarantee the Lord to be right there with you all the time, helping you through the afflictions of life. This proving, His grace is sufficient for thee.

The year was 1978. My young family and I were attending Apostolic Temple United Pentecostal Church in Lake Charles, Louisiana. Our Pastor was Dr. M. D. Treece. (He is the greatest pastor in the world.) I seemingly was on a fast climb of success in the business world. (Not going into all the business details.) Seemingly quicker than I had made my climb to success, there was a down-turn in my business. I had to quickly sell some of the assets I had and properties I had just acquired. The down-turn happened so suddenly that I could not seemingly overcome it. I immediately began to lose all my families possessions. I lost two brand new 1978 Ford pickup trucks; a new 1978 Lincoln Mark IV; a 1976 Buick Electra 225; a new 1978, 16' Tide Craft ski boat. I was able to sell my home before the foreclosure was finalized.

(In the middle of all this down-turn; to keep from losing everything I had worked for, I turned a portion of my business over to my partner. I gave him all of my existing inventory, office equipment, receivables and a small customer base. This was done with a handshake and a verbal understanding that I would be back in the business with him as soon as I could straighten my life and finances out.)

The end result was over two hundred eighty seven thousand dollars worth of judgments against me personally. I could not find a job at the time. No one would hire me; in fact I was treated by many as though I was too successful to work for them. There were others that treated me as though I had a plague, because I had been in competition with them and they were afraid.

I had managed to salvage some cash from some of the profits in the business, the selling of my home and the selling of some of my properties. But in all reality my family was broke. I had only been under the ministry of Bro. Treece a short while when all this began to happen in my life. I was too proud and also so humiliated to share my situation with anyone at the time. I also understood the house of the Lord was the place that I could go and lay my burdens before the Lord at the altar. It was also the place that I could receive refreshment, encouragement and strength. So I went to the house of the Lord for those purposes only; not to murmur and complain about the situation of my life.

Our lives as a young family really had taken a change. We moved out of a nice three bedroom home into a small two bedroom apartment. We lost all of our new automobiles, our status symbols so to speak. We were driving an older car that had belonged to my dad, then to our business and was about worn out. But the high-light of the moment was our spiritual life was starting to sparkle with fresh life. We became involved with every facet of the church. We sang in the choir, taught Sunday school, taught Bible studies, involved with bus ministry and outreach. We were faithful to church and became engulfed in the work of God in our church.

Sufficient Grace when Your Life is in the Sewer

A man and his wife at church approached me several times with a business proposition. They did not realize my personal financial problems. They were looking only at the successes of my past business dealings and wanted me as a partner in their new business venture. After many visits and after many times of my declining their offers, I explained my personal situation to them. This did not at all change or alter the fact they still wanted me and my wife as partners.

We finally made a deal and formed a Louisiana business corporation. We named the corporation J-San, Inc. We were now in a new business to both of us. We were in the sewer cleaning business; I was the "HMIC"(Head Man in Charge). We had just purchased the local "MR. ROOTER" franchise; you guessed it I was the new skin diver. I drove a green van with a smiling faced man on both sides and on the back door. But I can promise you, I as the driver was not smiling at all. I was smelly.

Your mind can not imagine the smell inside that stinking old rooter van. Some days the smells were worse than others. It really depended on the number of calls and how bad the calls themselves were.

<u>Writers note</u>: This part of my life is not meant to be derogatory towards anyone who does this type work for a living today. Nor is this meant to be derogatory towards the "MR. ROOTER" Companies or any other companies that clean sewers for a living.

First of all it is an honest living and the pay can be quiet good. But it was not something I had ever aspired or dreamed of doing. It was not something I even desired to do. I had never had it on my list of priorities to be known in Lake Charles, Calcasieu Parish, Louisiana, as "MR. ROOTER."

I will never forget my life as a routing, scooting sewer man; driving around in that stinking green sewer van. I was not a happy camper during that time.

As I look back in reminiscence, I really was not any different than anyone else who has difficulties. I began to cry out to God, as we all do when we are depressed or in deep turmoil and struggle.

I prayed as so many of us do when difficult situations come our way and things are not seemingly going well.

My prayers went something like this:
"Lord, don't you remember me? I attend Apostolic Temple in Lake Charles, Louisiana. Brother Marvin Treece is my pastor. Lord, I am faithful to my church. I attend prayer meetings, church services and revival services. I am involved in Bible studies, church outreach, black outreach and bus ministry. I pay my tithes, Lord. I give in the offerings and even support missions with PIM's. Why am I in this position Lord? Why me Lord?"

It seemed like the Lord was not listening to my prayers. The heavens seemed to be like solid brass. My prayers seemed to be in vain. Nothing seemed to change; we were still struggling and I was still in the sewer. I know that many of you feel or have felt like you have been cast into the sewers of life; you do not know why you are there; neither do you know how to get out and it seems like God is not with you in it at all.

I was called to an older home in Lake Charles one day. The home was eloquent in its style; it was built about three and a half feet off the ground. I was met at the door by an elderly lady. She explained to me the problem she was having with the sewer in her home. I told her I would have to go under her house and disconnect the main line and run my sewer cable from her house to the main sewer line. I told her not to run any water until I told her I was finished. I got my equipment under her house and disconnected the sewer line and had begun the process of rooting the line out with my electric eel. Just as I had gotten to the root of the problem, I heard a noise above me, glu-glu-gluug-gluug-gluug-gluug. As I looked up something from the above piping dissipated all over my face, head, chest and shoulders. For a man my size, actually a man any size, moving very rapidly under a house was next to impossible. I could not get away from that something that came from the sewer pipe above me.

Now for all of you reading this material, I do want you to understand I was a Christian when this happened. In fact I was a One God, tongue talking, Holy Ghost filled Apostolic Pentecostal. But I must admit at that very moment I was a very mad Pentecostal. I angrily got out from under that house and raced to the door and knocked so very loud and hard. (I had been taught by my parents to always show respect to my elders. But at that moment I forgot my upbringing, I had no respect at all for this elderly lady.) This lady gently opened her door as I yelled, "Ma'am didn't I tell you not to run water?" She responded so kindly, "Sir, I didn't run any water, you told me not to." I said, "ma'am what did you just do?" She said, "I just flushed the toilet."

Back under the house I went to complete this job. I was crying and praying all the time I was under the house. *"Why, Lord? I do not understand this at all. Don't you remember who I am? I attend Apostolic Temple; Bro. Marvin Treece is my pastor. Lord, I attend prayer meetings and all church services. I am involved in Bible studies, outreach, Sunday school and bus ministry. Lord, I pay my tithes and offerings and even support PIM's for missions. Why am I in this position Lord?"*

Guess what? You probably guessed it, the Lord did not respond to my questions that day. He still to this very day has never told me why I was there? But I do understand this one thing now. While I was struggling under this home as "MR. ROOTER" the Lord was there with me through it all.

I was called to the Town of Westlake sewer plant. The line that flowed from the main sewer tank to the river was plugged up. The city workers had dug a deep hole around the 20 inch pipeline and valve that came out of the bottom of this sewer tank. In the top of the pipe they had cut a 6 inch hole so that the cable from my electric eel could go into the line and work.

The cable went at least fifty feet into the line and got hung up. I pulled with all my might and strength and could not get the cable free. About that time the dinner bell rang for the town workers. I told these workers that I was going to lunch also, but while I was gone I said, "Do not open the valve from the tank, because it would fill that hole I was standing in with some stinking stuff." I had to get my cable out of that line before they opened the valve and tried the line again. To my amazement, when I returned from lunch, the valve had been opened. The hole I had been standing down in to work was now full of stuff. (*I am not going to identify this word stuff; I will leave it to your imagination to figure it out.*) I did not say much, I put on my rubber boots and rubber gloves then stepped out onto that 20 inch pipeline, in the stuff. I reached down and got a good grip on my cable and pulled on it, but nothing happened. I pulled a second time, still nothing happened. The Town workers were all standing around laughing and poking fun and I was getting just a little bit angry. I pulled on the cable this time with all my might and strength. To my amazement the cable came loose and when it did so did I. I slipped off the 20 inch pipeline and fell chest deep into the stuff. The men from the Town of Westlake were all laughing even more now. I must admit that I was openly crying with deep anger and utter disbelief that this could have happened to me. At that moment I did not care who heard me or who saw me. I began to speak to the Lord, something like this, *"Why me Lord? Don't you remember me? I go to Apostolic Temple; Bro Marvin Treece is my pastor. Lord, I attend prayer meetings, I am faithful to church services, I am involved in outreach, Bible studies and even goes on bus ministry. I pay my tithes, give in offerings and even support PIM's for missions. Why am I in this position?"*

The heavens seemed to be brass that day and it did not seem that God was even listening to me. I went home and had to take my clothes off outside. I showered for such a long, long time before I was clean enough to do anything. I had to literally burn my boots and clothes.

Life as "MR. ROOTER" was not a pleasant time for me. My children, who were just starting to Middle School at the time, would not let me take them all the way to their school in the Mr. Rooter van. They did not like the ridicule from their friends about their dad's job. My wife often met me at the carport and would make me take my rooter clothes off before I went in our apartment. Our German shepherd dog even bit me one night, mistaking me for an intruder. A State Trooper stopped me early one morning. He took my driver's license and walked around the van. When he got back to where I was standing, He said, "Do you have to drive this van all day?" I answered, "Yes, sometimes I drive it for twenty four hours a day, because I am always on call." He handed me my driver's license back saying, "Anyone who has to ride in something like this all day, deserves a break." There were a few good things to be remembered, even while I was in the sewer.

Oh how I cried and prayed while I drove that old green rooter van. Believe it or not, it was while I was in the sewers that I developed a closer relationship with God. It was in these times of distress that I began to understand a little more about God's Grace; realizing His Grace is sufficient, for even me.

Meeting Leon:

As I sat in the old green van, parked in front of "Marcantels Grocery Store" just after daybreak one dreary morning, something strange happened.

You must get a vision of the conditions, it was cold and raining outside, it was grim. I had gotten an early morning call and after finishing it, I stopped by the store to get a cake and chocolate milk, which I did regularly.

As I sat in the van eating the cake and drinking the chocolate milk, there was a knock on my driver's side window. It startled me, because I had not noticed anyone come to the van. I rolled the window down, and there stood a short, stocky black man. In his hand he was holding a small red "New Testament." He said to me, *"Sir as I went into the store the Lord spoke to me. He told me you were the man that would teach me His Word."* The young man went on to say something like this, *"I love God with all my heart, but I can hardly read or write. I go to church and hear preaching, but I am missing so much. I want to be able to read the Bible with a clear understanding."*

Now you must understand, at that moment I could not see the handy work of God in all that was taking place. I was not in a real good mood that morning; but at that time of my life I was never in a good mood, and I was so caught up in my own problems that I could not see the handy work of God. I said to this young man, *"If you don't mind riding in this stinking van, then I will read the Bible to you today."* To my amazement he went to the passenger side of the van and got in and did not seem to be bothered by the stench at all.

Every morning for the next two weeks (with the exception of the weekends), I would pick Leon up and he would ride with me in my old green van. Between my rooter calls, I would stop and take out two Bibles. I would turn both Bibles to the same chapter and would read to Leon. I would read a verse or two and he and I would discuss what I just read. I did not realize what was happening to us at this time. Leon was learning to understand the written Word of God and learning how to read. I was being changed, even though I did not realize it at the time. I was growing stronger in my knowledge and understanding of the Word of God, and I was getting my mind off my own problems at the time. I did not realize it at that time, but God was doing a work through me. I was now reflecting Jesus Christ through my own life, something that I had not been doing for a great while. The Grace of God was surely sufficient for me and Leon at this time and neither one of us realized what was really happening.

So many of us who claim to be Christians get caught up in our own struggles of life, all we can see is our own problems. Therefore our vision is cloudy and we fail to see the multitudes of distraught, hurting people that we pass every single day. We most often fail to let God's grace reflect through us and in living like this, and the world around us misses their opportunity to experience the saving Grace of Jesus Christ.

At 7:00 am one morning I picked Leon up at his house, he said, "Bro. Man," I want to take you by my mom's to introduce you to her. He said, "She is a unique lady, but I want you to be prepared." I said, "Leon I will be delighted to meet your mother." Leon began to describe his mother to me. "She attends Saint Matthews Baptist Church and is faithful to every service. She has a station wagon that she fills up with ladies and children from the community and takes them all to church. I love my mom he went on, but she is different than the rest of the people she goes to church with. I said, "Leon, do not worry, I will like your mother." He said, "I know that you will, but I need to warn you, so you will understand, she is different." "She raises her hands when she prays at church." I said, "I can deal with that, Leon." "But, she prays out-loud." I said, "Leon, I can deal with that." "But, she claps her hands when she gets happy." I said, "I can deal with that." "But, she will dance in the aisle sometimes." I said, "I can deal with that." "But Bro. Man, she speaks with other tongues." I said, great Leon, I can deal with all of that." By this time we were now at her home. When we walked into her kitchen, she was seated at a small table eating her breakfast. She looked directly at me with amazement in her eyes. Both of her hands went up as she pointed out me and exclaimed, "You are the man." I jumped back and said, "It couldn't be me, I have never been in this community before." She said, "You don't understand. I was in my prayer closet a couple weeks ago. I have been praying for many years for God to send someone to this community that will teach our people the truth. I do not know whether, I had a vision or a dream; but while I was praying God showed me a man that would come to our community and teach our people His Word. My brother, you were that man. I accepted her challenge. The very next Monday night I started teaching Bible study in her home. It became a Monday night tradition, prayer meeting and Bible study at her Michigan Avenue home, 7:00 pm.

For the next eight and a half to nine years, I taught Bible study in that community. Not only did people of that community attend the Bible study, but there were several folks from other communities that attended. At the peak of the Bible study we averaged fifty-four people in the Bible study.

Not only did I teach the Bible study in their community, I taught in many of their local churches. I taught in their local community camp meeting and in many of their other community gatherings. I saw God move in such a very special way. Several folks who were in that community were baptized in Jesus name and were filled with the Baptism of the Holy Ghost. Leon, can read the Bible, can quote more scripture than I can. He is actually is a good speaker.

I look back and see the "Grace of God" through all of this, like I had never seen before. I now understand if God had left me on the mountain we call success in life, the place where I could have thought I was somebody. I would not have been willing to go to that community and teach the Word of God to that community. When God allowed me to go to the bottom myself, to the place where I understood I could not make it without Him, to the place I realized I was a no body. It was then that I allowed Him to use me to help these very dear and precious people. If I would have met Leon, when I was a success in business I would probably never helped him as I did; but the Lord allowed me to go to the sewers of our community so I was willing to help him. It was there, when I was at the bottom, I for the first time of my life began to understand the grace of God, and God began to use me. I can honestly say with all of my heart, "God's Grace Is Sufficient," for you and me.

There are times in our lives that we as saints of God feel that we are all alone and God has forgotten us. We pray and it seems like He does not hear; the heavens are brass, our words seemingly echo back to our ears. It is during these times that we need to understand our God is there with us. Most often we do not understand these afflictions of life that we encounter; but if our faith is in Jesus Christ, our Lord and Savior; if our trust is in Him, we will have no doubt that He knows exactly what He is doing. His grace is sufficient for every trial, every calamity, all troubles, sorrows, pain and grief.

When your back is against the wall, you have nowhere to turn, and it seems like you are finished; just remember how it was when his back was against the old rugged cross. He had been publicly ridiculed by his own people. One of His chosen disciples had betrayed Him. He had been lied about, mocked, ridiculed, and publicly humiliated. He was tried in a mock trial by His peers. He was slapped, spat upon, stripped and publicly beaten. He had the heavy cross placed upon His shoulders and had to drag it up the hill called Calvary. They placed a crown of thorns on top of His head, nailed His hands and feet to the cross and pierced His side with a spear. It was just before He died He spoke these words, "Father forgive them for they know not what they do," and finally He said, "it is finished" He bowed His head and gave up the ghost and died like a criminal of that day would die. He was then buried in a borrowed grave. On the third day he arose with great victory, to proclaim to those who would willingly follow him, that "His grace was sufficient." Through all of this, we as saints of God should let His grace reflect through our life, everywhere we are.

An old song that we sang when I was a young person at our local assembly:

> *"Trials dark on every hand, and we can not understand*
> *all the ways that God would lead us, to that blessed promise*
> *land; but he guides us with his eyes, if we follow till we die*
> *and we'll understand it better by and by."*

We will never understand all the things we face in this life. If we will keep our mind on the Lord; our hearts fixed on things above. Continue to walk by faith, and do the will of God; understanding his grace is sufficient. Then we will one day hear him say, "well done."

> II Corinthians 4:6(a)-10 KJV, Paul preaching, *"For God, who commanded the light to shine out of darkness, hath shined in our hearts... But we have this treasure in earthen vessels that the excellency of the power may be of God, and not of us.*
> *We are troubled on every side, yet not distressed; we are perplexed, but not in despair; Persecuted, but not forsaken; cast down, but not destroyed;*
> *Always bearing about in the body the dying of the Lord Jesus, that the life also of Jesus might be made manifest in our body."*

In my opinion, grace is the ability that God gives individuals to fulfill His will in their lives. Whatever His will and purpose for your life God will give you grace sufficient to do it. Do not get offended by the treatment you are receiving from this cold, cruel, dark world. Remember, if you are a child of God, this world is not your home, you are just passing through. Saints of God, we are pilgrims and strangers, just passing through this old world. There is only one place with no hurts, no pains, no calamities, no trouble, no afflictions, and no death:

"Heaven, our happy home above.
Heaven, land of peace and love.
Heaven, that city where the lamb is the light.
Heaven, where there will be no more night.
Heaven, a place that he has gone to prepare
for the saved and free.
Oh, how I want to go there."

Ephesians 2:8 KJV,
"For by grace are ye saved through faith; and that not of yourselves: it is the gift of God?"

Do not get caught up in seeing how great other folks seemingly have it now and how bad it seems to be in your life. Let your heart, mind and sight be fixed on Christ Jesus and nothing else. When your heart is fixed on Him, you will understand more and more about God's grace. When your mind is stayed on Him and your eyes are fixed on Him, He will begin to shine deep into your heart. It will be then that you will reflect Him through your life and living. Then the hurting world that is around you will see and begin to understand His Grace is sufficient, even for them.

Writer's Note: In this I tell of all my financial problems during 1978. These financial burdens were a part of my life and affected my family for approximately four years. God helped us during that time providing all of our needs. The end result was that all of my debts were taken care of and God replaced everything we lost and so much more. His Grace has been, and still is sufficient for me and my family.

Acts 16:16-25 KJV,

And it came to pass, as we went to prayer, a certain damsel possessed with a spirit of divination met us, which brought her masters much gain by soothsaying The same followed Paul and us, and cried, saying, These men are the servants of the highest God, which shew unto us the way of salvation. And this did her many days. But Paul, being grieved, turned and said to the spirit, I command thee in the name of Jesus Christ to come out of her. And he came out the same hour. And when her masters saw that the hope of their gains was gone, they caught Paul and Silas, and drew them into the marketplace unto the rulers, And brought them to the magistrates, saying, These men, being Jews, do exceedingly trouble our city, And teach customs, which are not lawful for us to receive, neither to observe, being Romans. And the multitude rose up together against them: and the magistrates rent off their clothes, and commanded to beat them. And when they had laid many stripes upon them, they cast them into prison, charging the jailor to keep them safely: Who, having received such a charge, thrust them into the inner prison, and made their feet fast in the stocks. And at midnight Paul and Silas prayed, and sang praises unto God: and the prisoners heard them.

Chapter Two

"Walking By Faith"

As children of God, there are times in our daily walk with the Lord that it just seems that Satan can do with us as he pleases. We must all get a good understanding about problems about worries and cares. Sometimes the load will seem so hard for you to bear. Satan will falsely accuse you for things you have not thought of doing, let alone even done. Satan will do everything he can to affect your income. When your bank account and pocketbook are empty, this will put a strain on your life and your family. Satan will do everything he can to destroy your health, or the health of one of your family members. When you or a family member is ill or afflicted, this really does cause much stress. Satan is working overtime to destroy our families, causing many good couples to bust up and say it is over. This affects the children the rest of their lives, oh what stress.

I want to point out something very important. Satan is not as concerned with your family's welfare as it seems. He is not concerned with your money and possessions. He really does not care how well you and your family get along. He could care less if any of you are sick or well. What Satan is really after is your faith in God. He uses all these other hurts and losses to get you in a position of despondency so he can move in and steal your faith.

If Satan can steal your faith, he knows that you are now defenseless. You are no longer a threat to him or any of the evil spirits of this present world. You are then of very little value at that moment in the work of God

Hebrews 11:6 KJV,
"But without faith it is impossible to please him: for he that cometh to God must believe that he is, and that he is a rewarder of them that diligently seek him."

The Apostle Paul had a night vision in Acts 16:9. In that vision a man from Macedonia stood before him and begged him to come to Macedonia and help them. Paul being the man of God that he was immediately began to get himself in position and gathering everything to gather to go to Macedonia. He understood this was God calling him to go into this region of the world and to preach the gospel to these people. He understood God had a people prepared to receive and accept this great gospel as truth and to be saved.

Acts 16:9-10 KJV,
"And a vision appeared to Paul in the night; There stood a man of Macedonia, and prayed him, saying, Come over into Macedonia, and help us. And after he had seen the vision, immediately we endeavored to go into Macedonia, assuredly gathering that the Lord had called us for to preach the gospel unto them."

Paul got everything gathered up and took with him a man by the name of Silas. Paul understood this was an urgent cry from the people of Macedonia for this message of salvation. They went as rapidly as they could go and when they had arrived in the city of Philippi, the largest city of that area in Macedonia, they stayed there for several days with no action at all. On the Sabbath day, Paul and Silas went a little way outside the city to a riverbank. This is the place that they had been told that people gathered for a regular prayer meeting. They sat down to speak with some women who had gathered there to pray.

One of these was Lydia, who was from the city of Thyatira. She was a merchant of expensive purple cloth, who worshiped God. As she listened to Paul and Silas, the Lord opened her heart, and she accepted the preaching of the Apostle Paul. She was baptized along with other members of her household, and she asked us to be guests in her home. Lydia said to Paul, "If you agree that I am a true saint of God, I would love for you to come and stay in my home." After much urging Paul and Silas agreed to stay in the home of Lydia.

Sufficient Grace when Your Life is in the Sewer

On one of the days as Paul and Silas were going down to the place of prayer, they were met by a demon-possessed slave girl. This girl was a soothsayer or fortune-teller, who earned a lot of money for her masters. She followed Paul and those who were with them, shouting, "These men are servants of the Most High God, and they have come to tell you about salvation." This went on several days until Paul got so frustrated that he turned and said to the demon within her, "I command you in the name of Jesus Christ to come out of her." And instantly that demon came out and left her.

Her masters' hopes of wealth were now shattered, so they grabbed Paul and Silas and dragged them before the authorities at the marketplace. "The whole city was in an uproar because of these Jews!" They said to the authorities, "These men are teaching customs that are illegal for us Romans to practice." The officials ordered them stripped and publicly beaten. Paul and Silas were severely beaten, and then they were thrown into prison. The jailer was ordered to make sure they did not escape. He put them into the inner cell, or dungeon, and clamped their feet in the stocks.

Can you only imagine how Paul and Silas must have felt? They felt as if they were following the call of God. They were doing the perfect will of God, taking this message of truth to a lost people who had no one to preach to them. I am sure that Satan was really enjoying this. Oh how happy he must have been, the men that God had sent to deliver Macedonia from his clutches were in stocks and chains in the inner most prison of Philippi.

My wife and I were traveling evangelists, several years ago. On our first trip to the Whitehorse, Yukon, Canada. There were several people at the pastor's house. We men were in the dining area of the house with the pastor. The ladies were all in the living area of the house talking with the pastor's wife. There were no partitions or walls between us, so we could hear from each room. The ladies were on the subject of berry picking. Sandy (my wife), has never gone berry picking in her life and I wondered how she was going to get out of this. She questioned, "aren't there bears out there where you ladies are going?" The pastors wife responded, "sister, we are going directly into bear territory," "actually we are going to where they are feeding as they come out of hibernation." Sandy said, "What do you do if you encounter a bear, while you are picking berries?" The pastor's wife got up out of her chair, went down a flight of stairs to her basement and came back with a high-powered rifle strapped over her shoulder. She patted the rifle and said, "I just take my weapon of assurance with me, if a bear does come charging after me, I raise my rifle up and shoot him down."

The reason these ladies had little to no fear when they went into the wild to pick berries is because they took their weapons of assurance with them. This is the way it must be with us spiritually. We must not fear and tremble every day of our life. We must carry our weapon of assurance with us everywhere we go. Yes, every day of our life we are working for the Lord in Satan's territory. We must have our faith with us at all times, so we can run him off and literally defeat him.

We must remember the truth of all that matters in our life. It is true, that faith has healed so many that are sick. Faith has even raised some that were dead. It has been faith that opened eyes of the blind and cause the lame to leap. Faith has supplied our every need. Faith has gotten us to where we are as individuals today. It is because of our faith and trust in Jesus Christ that we are even saved today. Yet with all that we can see with our natural eye and all that we remember and know. So many of us, as saints of God live so helpless; we live so lifeless; we live in fear and terror of Satan. We must put our total trust in our Lord and Savior Jesus Christ, understand He is the power that is above every power? He is a great big awesome and wonderful God.

Faith is not a crutch. It is not something that we lean on, just to hobble and cripple our way through our daily living. Faith is our shield. A shield was a part of the battle armor that was worn during the Old and New Testament times. Some had a shield that was carried by an armor bearer. The armor bearer always stayed in a position so the warrior could get behind the shield if a volley of arrows or darts were fired from the enemy. But the shield I like to read about, and I believe is the one the Bible is describing our faith to be like, was the shield that was made specifically for the individual warrior. The shield was balanced to rest properly at his side until needed and then he would place it on his forearm as protection against the enemy. This type shield was also razor sharp on the bottom edge. The warrior had a sword in one hand and a shield on the other arm and he could actually cut the enemy with either weapon. Therefore the shield was both a defensive and offensive weapon. Faith is a weapon that we use in our spiritual battles. We can stop the fiery darts shot at us by Satan or his demons or we can use it to cut asunder the evil spirits that come against us often.

How do we develop our shield of faith, so that it will be well balanced and made just for our needs. We get involved with the Word of God through reading, study, hearing preachers preach the Word.

We begin to hear the Word, know the Word, Love the Word, through the Word we trust the Lord.

Romans 10:17 KJV,
*"So then faith cometh by hearing,
and hearing by the word of God."*

One thing that I have learned about faith, it is not transient. The faith that is with you today, will be with you tomorrow. It will be with you next week. It will be with you next month. It will be with you next year. It is lasting abiding faith.

1 Corinthians 13:13 New Living Translation ®,
*"Three things will last forever—faith, hope,
and love—and the greatest of these is love."*

You and I who are saints of God do not have to worry or fear. We do not have to doubt we can relax in the loving arms of Jesus Christ our God and Savior. We can enjoy life and living. We can enjoy our salvation, because we understand and know our God has never failed us and He never will. We can have faith in Him and trust Him with everything in our life.

I have Christian people all the time; I am talking about saints of God that tell me. Preacher you just do not understand my situation. I had a close call the other day, nearly had a wreck that could have taken my life. I am scared to death. You do not understand how sick my child has been preacher. Fever has been so high, we are so fearful that we just do not know what to do. Preacher my financial situation has been so terrible. I am so broke that I just do not know what to do. I am about to lose everything and you want me to have faith? Perhaps you that are reading this manuscript at this moment are like these that are written about. It is true; perhaps, I do not understand your situation. But I do understand that God loves you. I do know that God was in that automobile and kept you from having your wreck, you need to thank Him and start trusting Him. I do know that God is the one that has touched your child's fevered brow and for that you need to thank, praise Him and trust Him. I do know that in spite of your financial crises, God has supplied your needs and fed your family for that there should be some thanks and trust.

Come on saint of God, let's you and I pick up our shield of faith and start trusting our Lord through it all. You and I may not understand all that is happening in our lives at this moment. I have learned there are many things I have been through, I have never been able to figure out the reasons or the why's. But through it all I do know that God wants us to understand He is there with us all the time. He also wants us to understand if we continue to have faith in Him and trust Him, He will see us through it all to victory.

There are so many Christian people who walk by feeling when it comes to serving the Lord. Feelings should have nothing to do with our faith. If you are one that walks by feeling alone, the devil will have you as nervous as a termite in a yo-yo. You won't know if you are coming are going because you will always be so confused. Feelings are like a sailboat that is blown by every wind and tossed to and fro. But faith is like a mighty ocean liner, that no matter what the winds, it just keeps forging straight ahead.

2 Corinthians 5:7 KJV,
"(For we walk by faith, not by sight:" ☺

There is an old song that the elders sang when I was a lad and even into my teenage years.

*"I'm feeling mighty fine,
I've got heaven on my mind,
O, don't know I want to go
where the milk and honey flow,
there's a light that always shines,
down inside this heart of mine,
I've got heaven, heaven on my mind,
and now I'm feeling mighty fine."*

I would love to get up every morning, be able to go through every day, feeling fine. But it does not always work like that. Sometimes I do not feel fine. Sometimes I feel bad. Sometimes I feel sick. Sometimes I feel down and despondent. Sometimes I feel discouraged even somewhat depressed. Sometimes I feel weak and weary. But my feelings do not weaken my faith. My feelings do not change the power of God. Saints we must get our minds fixed on the fact our God is an awesome, all powerful and mighty God. How we feel should have no affect on our faith. We should simply trust God, because He is God. If we will forever settle that in our mind we will be able to trust Him through the good times as well as the bad times of our life.

When you and I of this modern age read about our heroes of faith in the Bible, we often think of them as Herculean in stature and might. We think of them as we would the Hulk, when they flex their muscles we think their shirts would tear and rip. We simply think they were super-humans. You know they were people of steel. In our mindset, they did not feel the pains that we feel; face the sorrows of life that we face; they were just so strong and different than we are today. But my Bible lets me know they were men of like passion as we. Therefore when they were sick, they felt bad just like we do. When they had pains in their bodies it hurt just like the pains in our bodies. But the Bible says they lived by faith. The difference between their day and ours, they could only trust God by their own instincts and instruction. We can trust Him because His Spirit dwells within us through the power of the Holy Ghost and also we do have His written Word to read and get instruction and encouragement from daily.

If our hero of faith, Noah, would show up at our church on a Sunday morning, I believe he would walk all the way down to the front row and sit right in front of the pulpit for the entire service. Once we realized who he was we would probably begin to question him. Noah how do you feel today? He would probably answer something like this. "I'm not feeling so well I am almost six hundred years old and I am building an ark. I am not as strong as I was in my younger years. I have calluses on my hands and my feet, I am starting to get tired and weary. "Well Noah, why don't you just go home, take it easy get a little rest." "No, I must continue to build the ark." "But Noah, why do you have to work so hard to build that old boat, we have never seen rain here before?" Noah responds, God said, He is going to send rain. He will destroy the earth by flood and the only escape is the ark that I am building. It is for the saving of my family. So by faith I will go saw some more wood, drive some more nails use some more pitch. I am not building this ark by feeling. I am building it by faith, because I trust the Word of God. And I am working to save my family." We know the end result.

Hebrews 11:7 KJV,
"By faith Noah, being warned of God of things not seen as yet, moved with fear, prepared an ark to the saving of his house; by the which he condemned the world, and became heir of the righteousness which is by faith."

Now if Job would also show up at our church on Sunday morning, he would take his seat right next to Noah on the front pew. Once we figured out who he was we would ask him, "how do you feel?" I believe there would be a little snarl on his face as he answered that question. "You mean to tell me, you have the audacity to ask me how I feel. I feel like warmed over death. I have boils on my feet, on my seat, on my head, on my back, on my belly, between my toes, they are up my nose and even inside my ears. I am a bloody mass of corruption and you ask me how I feel? I am in an awful shape. My children are now dead and gone, my livestock and possessions stolen and gone. My wife who has been through as much as I have has told me to give up, to go ahead and curse God and die. I told her not to think like a foolish woman. God gives and God takes away, blessed be His Holy Name. My friends are falsely accusing me of sin and you ask me how I feel?" Saints of God through all of Jobs troubles, trials and many losses he never wavered in his faith.

Job 13:15-16 KJV,
"Though he slay me, yet will I trust in him:
but I will maintain mine own ways before him.
He also shall be my salvation: for an hypocrite
shall not come before him."

Job 19:25-26 KJV,
"For I know that my redeemer liveth, and that
he shall stand at the latter day upon the earth:
And though after my skin worms destroy this body,
yet in my flesh shall I see God:"

Job 42:12-13 KJV,

"So the Lord blessed the latter end of Job more than his beginning: for he had fourteen thousand sheep, and six thousand camels, and a thousand yoke of oxen, and a thousand she asses. He had also seven sons and three daughters."

Remember we left Paul and Silas in a bad predicament in this manuscript. Let's go back and find them. The officials had ordered them to be stripped and publicly beaten. Paul and Silas were severely beaten, and then they were thrown into prison. The jailer was ordered to make sure they did not escape. He put them into the cell, or dungeon, and clamped their feet in the stocks.

We can only imagine how Paul and Silas must have felt. They felt as if they were following the call of God, doing the perfect will of God, taking this message of truth to a lost people who had no one to preach to them. Then around midnight Paul and Silas were praying and singing hymns to God, and the other prisoners were listening because they could hear. While they were singing and praising the Lord, suddenly, there was a massive earthquake, and the prison was shaken to its foundations. Every door was opened, and the chains of every prisoner fell off! Can you understand the astonishment of all the prisoners in those cells?

The jailer, who had been charged by the officials to keep these prisoners secured in this jail, woke up to see the prison doors wide open. He was so stunned by what he saw. He also assumed the prisoners had escaped, so he drew his sword to kill himself. He was going to take his own life. He knew the officials were going to charge him with neglect of duty, because these prisoners had escaped while under his watch.

The Apostle Paul shouted to him, "Stop! Do not kill yourself! We are all here!" The jailer called for a light. He then ran to the dungeon and fell down trembling before Paul and Silas. Then the jailer brought them out and asked, "Sirs, what must I do to be saved?" They replied, "Believe in the Lord Jesus and you will be saved, along with everyone in your household."

Then Paul and Silas spoke the word of the Lord, sharing with him and with all who lived in his household. Even though this was taking place after midnight, the jailer had them cared for and their wounds washed and cleansed.

Now the exciting part of this entire story takes place after they were beaten and thrown in jail. Paul and Silas had come to Philippi because of the Apostle Paul's night vision. They came to find that man that was hungry for God and searching for truth. They would have never found him if they would not have been thrown into prison. But here they were the jail was opened, the jailer had asked about salvation. The jailer and his family had taken care of their wounds. Without any hesitation the jailer and everyone in his household were immediately baptized. Paul and Silas were brought into his house and they were fed. The jailer and his entire household rejoiced because they all believed in God. All of this took place because Paul and Silas were following the will of God.

Even though things had not worked out the way they thought they would. Even though their life was uncomfortable and they were being falsely accused they continued in prayer and praising to God. These men proved to all of us, we who are called by God cannot, must not walk by feelings. We must walk by faith. We have been called by God, chosen to fulfill His perfect will and we must continue walking by faith.

The next day the city officials sent someone to tell the jailer, "Let those men go." So the jailer told Paul, "The city officials have said you and Silas are free to leave our city now and to go in peace." Paul replied to his new friend, "They have publicly beaten us without a trial. Then put us in prison under your watchful eye and placed us in chains and stocks. Both of us are Roman citizens. Now they have sent us word we are free to go in peace and they want us to leave secretly? I don't think so! If they want us to leave they are going to have to come and release us themselves." When this report was brought to the city officials, they all became alarmed. They had not taken time to even find out that Paul and Silas were citizens of Rome. These officials came to the jail and apologized to them. They then escorted Paul and Silas out of the jail and begged them to leave their city.

The eternal results of Paul and Silas walking by faith and trusting in the Lord are so very many. By keeping their eyes on the Lord and not on their personal circumstances they found the man that God had brought to Paul in a night vision. He and his whole household were baptized by Paul and Silas and when they left that city they left it in the hands of some followers and believers of Jesus Christ. These people were now filled with the Holy Ghost; the Spirit of God was now present in their lives and their city. What a wonderful ending, because Paul and Silas were "***Walking By Faith***."

Exodus 3:11 KJV,
*"And Moses said unto God, Who am I, that
I should go unto Pharaoh, and that I should bring
forth the children of Israel out of Egypt?"*

CHAPTER THREE

"Who Am I?"

Writer's notes: *My wife and I still call Apostolic Temple home and Dr. Marvin Treece and his wonderful son Rev. Rick Treece are still our pastors. These two great preachers and their families are some of the greatest Christians I have ever been associated with. I count them all as dear friends. Everyone at Apostolic Temple we count you as some of the greatest people that have ever affected our lives. Thank you all for loving us so dearly during all of our struggles.*

If ever there was a preacher, who has written a book or even stood behind a pulpit and felt inadequate, it is the one that is writing this manuscript. Personally I have battled with myself over my entire lifetime. I have battled with my inadequacies, with my inferior complexes, with the fact I simply do not have the abilities to do the work of God. But it was after many hard lessons in life, much struggle and turmoil, much suffering, and pain, and after so many failures of life. I found myself in the desert, (so to speak.) I was all alone, nowhere to go, nowhere to run, nowhere to hide. I was in a position I had to listen and then talk to God.

It is my opinion, that God does not immediately put individuals on a pedestal in leadership when He first calls them. I do believe that everyone who is called and chosen by God, have been called for a specific purpose. I feel that God leads every one of us that He has chosen through a process of development and training. So very often, many of us fail the course. We then have to take the course again and again. I personally have failed many times and have had to take the courses that God is bringing me through over again.

Moses was chosen and ordained by God from his very birth, to lead the children of Israel out of Egypt's bondage. God did not immediately set Moses up in that position of leadership. But, through a series of training and development God brought him through the school of life's hard knocks.

Often when we read the Bible, we fail to see all the circumstances which have lead to the victorious events. We have a tendency of shouting over the successes we read about. All the while failing to notice the steps they took to get them to these victories. Because of the way we read these stories we often miss the lesson they learned and fail to see all the failures they encountered in getting to the point of victory. Most often we look only at the end results of success and victory. We fail to see the steps God put them through to develop them.

Moses was no different than any other human being. He had qualities and abilities that had to be developed by God. Because God understood there were challenges that he was going to face as the leader of the Children of Israel.

Most of us who are alive in this era of time want the success and the victories right now. But few of us are willing to be developed the way that God wants to develop us. If you and I are not willing to go to God's schooling of preparation, we will never reach the peak of success in our walk with God. Success with God is not instantaneous. Success with God is developed by God in each of us as individuals. You and I are called by God, we are chosen by God and we will be developed by God.

You know the story of Moses. How his mother concealed him until he was three months old. She then made him a little ark, or basket, and gently laid him in it. She took that ark to the bulrushes on the edge of the Nile River. Pharaoh's daughter came to the Nile with some of her maidens to bathe. She saw the ark and sent her maid to get it. When the ark was opened, she was moved with compassion because the baby boy was crying. Pharaoh's daughter decided to keep the child and raise him as her own son. Unknowingly she let Moses own mother keep him and raise him until he no longer needed a maid.

Exodus 2:10 KJV,
"And the child grew, and she brought him unto Pharaoh's daughter, and he became her son. And she called his name Moses: and she said, because I drew him out of the water."

Moses was raised in the household of Pharaoh. He was taught the ways of Egypt. He ate from Pharaoh's table and was schooled at Pharaoh's schools. Moses had the best.

I personally differ with many theologians and preachers. I do not think that Moses knew any of the Hebrew ways. I do not believe he even had any inkling he was a Hebrew. Just because his mother had that little bit of time with him when he was a baby, many people say she put the Hebrew ways in him. I do not concur with that line of thinking. It was after he became a grown man before his heritage and lineage was revealed to him.

Many years later after Moses had grown up; he went out to visit his own people, the Hebrews. It was then that he saw how hard they were being forced to work. During his visit, he saw an Egyptian beating one of his fellow Hebrews. After looking in all directions to make sure no one was watching what was happening. Moses killed the Egyptian and hid the body in the sand. The very next day Moses went out to visit his people again. This time he saw two Hebrew men fighting. Moses asked the one that had seemed to be the instigator, "Why are you beating up your friend?" The man replied, "Who appointed you as our prince and judge? Are you going to kill me as

Sufficient Grace when Your Life is in the Sewer

you killed that Egyptian yesterday?" Then Moses was shook up, he was utterly afraid. He realized everyone must know what he had done.

As soon as Pharaoh heard what had happened, he sought to kill Moses. But Moses fled from Pharaoh and went to live in the land of Midian.

When Moses arrived in Midian, he sat down beside a well to rest himself for awhile. Now the priest of Midian had seven daughters who came as usual to draw water and fill the water troughs for their father's flocks.

Some other shepherds came and chased the girls and their flocks away from the water they had drawn. These shepherds were going to let their flocks drink the water the girls had drawn. Moses was resting beside the well and saw what was taking place, jumped up and rescued the girls from the shepherds.

He then ran the shepherds off. Then he drew water for the girl's flocks and watered them. Moses found favor in the home of Jethro, their father. He married the eldest daughter and stayed with them in Midian.

According to human reasoning, a sheep herder who is running for his life, who is tending to his father-in-laws sheep, does not seem like a good prospect to be a mighty deliverer. Being on the backside of a desert does not look like a good place to find a man who is called of God to deliver Israel from bondage. I am sure, that at that moment, Moses did not feel special either. Moses probably questioned as we often do. "What am I doing here?" "This is not what

I had in mind for my life." "I am a nobody, I am of no value, and I am a failure." "I will never be able to used for the glory of God"

I personally know about those type feelings. There have been numerous times in my own life that I felt like I was a one hundred percent failure. I had felt the call of God on my life as a young man. I had felt Gods anointing on my life so many times. But I was achieving nothing. My dreams were dissipating before me. My vision was so blurry. I felt so useless and so worthless and I had no way of changing my circumstances.

Many of you reading this manuscript can relate to this. You are feeling those same type pressures. You are not meeting your spiritual potential. You feel it is of no use to even try, because you are a failure. Surely God cannot use you, it is over God is through.

To me, there could be no worse place for one to find themselves, than where we find Moses, on the backside of a desert, tending another man's sheep. These sheep did not even belong to him.

Exodus 3:1 KJV,
"Now Moses kept the flock of Jethro his father in law, the priest of Midian: and he led the flock to the backside of the desert, and came to the mountain of God, even to Horeb."

Moses must have felt somewhat rejected and dejected. I am sure this was a lonely place for him

Sufficient Grace when Your Life is in the Sewer

to be. Defeated and disheartened, he kept the flocks day after day

I have learned something about walking with God.

Psalms 37:23-25 KJV,
"The steps of a good man are ordered by the Lord:
and he delighteth in his way.
Though he fall, he shall not be utterly cast down:
for the Lord upholdeth him with his hand.
I have been young, and now am old;
yet have I not seen the righteous forsaken,
nor his seed begging bread."

If you are called by God, there is a purpose in every step of your way. God has placed His approval on your life through His anointing. You may not like the position you have found yourself in. You may not even like being on the backside of the desert. You may even question, "Why do I find myself in this position?"

Moses had to leave the land of Egypt, the life of being groomed to be a Pharaoh, to run for his life to the backside of the desert, simply to get to the Mountain of God.

Exodus 3:1 KJV,
"Now Moses kept the flock of Jethro his father in law, the priest of Midian: and he led the flock to the backside of the desert, and came to the **mountain of God***, even to Horeb."*

God has got to get each and every one of us to that place in our life, where He has our undivided attention. He has to get us to a place of no distractions. That is why He brings us to the backside of nowhere. Yes, to the backside of a desert, so to speak, so He can have our undivided attention. We find Moses on the backside of the desert, at the mountain of God. Now God has his undivided attention.

Too often God cannot get our attention when everything is comfortable and good. He has to get us out of our comfort zone. Get us away from everything and even everyone we know, get us all alone by our self. He has to get us in a position that we feel our need of Him before He can really talk with us.

God could not use Moses as long as he thought He was somebody, while he had aspirations of being a success in Egypt. God had to get Moses to the place he understood he was a no body, before he could get him to stop long enough to speak to him.

Some of you understand what I am writing about. At this very moment, you feel you are on the backside of the desert all alone, by yourself. But the good news of all this is, the backside of the desert is not the end for you. It is here that you will find your real purpose in living for God, even the purpose for your life. It is here that you will begin to have a deeper walk with the Lord. It is here on the backside of the desert, that God speaks and you listen.

It was on the backside of the desert that Moses had his first encounter with the supernatural power of God.

Exodus 3:2 KJV,
"And the angel of the Lord appeared unto him in a flame of fire out of the midst of a bush: and he looked, and, behold, the bush burned with fire, and the bush was not consumed."

If you are on the backside of the desert, in that place called nowhere, do not give up. There is a purpose for your being where you are. God does have a plan for your life. Just wait God is about to give you your next instructions.

Writers note: *God's instruction will always line up with His written Word.*

As you read this manuscript, take a moment to imagine with me. Here was Moses, on the backside of the desert, just another monotonous long hot day, in the life of a sheep herder. All of a sudden something phenomenal happens; a bush begins to burn, but it does not burn up. (*According to commentaries and secular writings alike, a blazing bush in this setting is not uncommon. Often in the desert areas of our world, when the temperatures get so very hot, a bush can reach a flash-point and blaze in an instant.*)

But the phenomenon here was the bush was blazing, but was not being consumed. This did get Moses attention. Moses said to himself. "this is amazing why is that bush not burning up? This is something, I must go see it."

Exodus 3:4-5 KJV,
"And when the Lord saw that he turned aside to see, God called unto him out of the midst of the bush, and said, Moses, Moses. And he said, Here am I. And he said, Draw not nigh hither: put off thy shoes from off thy feet, for the place whereon thou standest is holy ground."

Moses for the first time in his life came face to face with the holiness of God. He came face to face with all the splendor, majesty and power of God. God was showing Moses the difference between the profane things of this present world and His holiness. Moses was brought to the place of separation. He was getting a feel of the real holiness of God. He saw the line that was drawn between the supernatural of God and the carnality of man.

Today there are so many who call themselves Christians who fail to see the majesty and splendor of God. We as humanity try to treat God as our little chummy buddy, like He is just our little supernatural pal. You know me and Jesus have our own thing going. God is not just our little buddy and pal, He is the power that is above all power. He is the King of kings and the Lord of lords. He is the Savior of the world, redeemer of mankind, our hope for tomorrow, the provider of everything. He is God all by Himself.

It was not until Moses saw the bush burning and stopped what he was doing to look. Then when he turned to get closer to this phenomenon, God spoke to him. God told him not to come any closer, stop where you are. Take your shoes off you are on holy ground.

The reason that so many people do not hear from God themselves, they never stop what they are doing long enough to turn and see the glory of God. If you want to hear from God, for yourself, you have got to first stop what you are doing. You must then turn toward the supernatural of God and meet Him on holy ground.

So many folks today, want to approach God any old way. People are just so casual when it comes to their approaching God. They think, because He is a God of love they can come into His presence as they would any casual individual. They fail to remember, our God is a holy God and we should reverence Him as such. When Moses heard that this was God speaking to him, he covered his face, he had so much reverence for God.

Exodus 3:6 KJV,
"Moreover he said, I am the God of thy father, the God of Abraham, the God of Isaac, and the God of Jacob. And Moses hid his face; for he was afraid to look upon God."

Saints of God, Christians please take notice: when you come face to face with God, please do not approach Him with such arrogance and pride. But approach Him with reverence and fear. Moses did not look upon Him, because He was God. He was the almighty. He was the holy God of his forefathers.

As Christian people today, you and I need an understanding about God like Moses had, an understanding of awe, fear and reverence. Many

Christians approach God so wrong today. They only worship Him, when He is providing their every want with good gifts and answering their prayers. We had best awaken ourselves and remember who He is. We best reverence Him and love Him simply because He is God. We must stop worshipping and praising Him only when He is doing things for us.

When Moses approached God, notice how God responded.

> Exodus 3:7-9 KJV,
> *"And the Lord said, I have surely seen the affliction of my people which are in Egypt, and have heard their cry by reason of their taskmasters; for I know their sorrows;And I am come down to deliver them out of the hand of the Egyptians, and to bring them up out of that land unto a good land and a large, unto a land flowing with milk and honey; unto the place of the Canaanites, and the Hittites, and the Amorites, and the Perizzites, and the Hivites, and the Jebusites. Now therefore, behold, the cry of the children of Israel is come unto me: and I have also seen the oppression wherewith the Egyptians oppress them."*

God was letting Moses understand He was listening and hearing the cries from His people and He has seen their oppressions from the Egyptians. I have come down for the purpose of delivering them from the Egyptians and to bring them into a good land that flows with milk and honey. Like the children of Israel of that day and time, we as saints of God get into our tough situations of life. We call on God, we cry and moan. But the heavens are brass, they are silent and we wonder where God is in all this. We must always remember, no matter what our trial or tribulation is, God is never asleep. He hears and knows our needs at all times.

Hebrews 13:5 (b) KJV,
"...for he hath said, I will never leave thee, nor forsake thee."

God was letting Moses know, that He was going to deliver them, but He had to have a man to go and bring them out of the land of bondage.

Exodus 3:10 KJV,
"Come now therefore, and I will send thee unto Pharaoh, that thou mayest bring forth my people the children of Israel out of Egypt."

When God does want to use us, to fulfill His will, and purpose, most of us feel inferior, timid, and shy. We just feel so inadequate, or just think ourselves to be unqualified.

Proverbs 29:25 KJV,
"The fear of man bringeth a snare: but whoso putteth his trust in the Lord shall be safe."

When we fear what another person can do to us, it will cause us to be bound. It will cause us to have an inferiority complex, thinking ourselves to be inferior to others. Also we will be so timid and shy binding us from ever accomplishing anything. We all face these kinds of feelings in our lives. But on the other hand, if we will give ourselves to the Lord and trust Him to use us for His will and purpose and do it with no fear we will be saved through this trust.

The first response Moses had, when God told him He wanted him to go to Pharaoh and bring the Children of Israel out of the land of Egypt.

> Exodus 3:11 KJV,
> *"And Moses said unto God, **Who am I**, that I should go unto Pharaoh, and that I should bring forth the children of Israel out of Egypt?"*

What Moses was trying to get across to God is the fact that God really did not know who He was dealing with at this moment. God you have made a big mistake, I am so unqualified. Also, he had a fear of going back into Egypt. Even though the older Pharaoh was now dead, his son knew Moses very well, and Moses had a fear that he might just take up his father's task of having Moses life. We can point our finger at Moses if we want to. We can preach about his fear all we want, but most of us are just like Moses. Our response is usually not any different. We then fold our hands, sit back and wait for God to handle every situation for us. Then when nothing happens, our families are still in bondage, we blame God for the problem.

God then told Moses that He would be with him. I will give you a sign that I am the one who has sent you. When you have brought the Children of Israel out of Egypt, you will bring them here to this very mountain to worship me. Moses was still not convinced that he could be used by God for this purpose. When I get to the Children of Israel and tell them the God of their ancestors has sent me to bring you out. Who am I to tell them has sent me, because they will ask me for His name.

Exodus 3:14 KJV,
"And God said unto Moses, I AM THAT I AM: and he said, Thus shalt thou say unto the children of Israel, I AM hath sent me unto you."

Remember Moses had been raised in Pharaoh's home. Moses had been schooled in Egypt and also raised in the Egyptian culture. Ancient Egyptian culture worshipped many different gods. They were taught that Pharaoh was one of their god's. When the elder Pharaoh died, and the younger Pharaoh replaced him, the older Pharaoh's spirit would go into the younger Pharaoh. They considered this to be a type of royal reincarnation. Because of this belief, the Egyptians often referred to the sitting Pharaoh as "I am." "I Am," is in present tense. This indicates a perpetual never-ending royal linage on the throne of Egypt. Moses having been raised as an Egyptian understood their culture well. This concept of Pharaoh being the "I Am," was part of his thinking and his tradition. This concept could have been part of what was restricting his faith at first.

Moses had asked God, "Who shall I say sent me?" God answered: "I AM THAT I AM." God was specific and to the point. You tell the Children of Israel, "that I AM hath sent me unto you." You tell them the King of kings has sent you. You tell them the only living King has sent you. You tell them the only King with a perpetual linage has sent you. You tell them the only I AM has sent you. I AM that only I AM.

In the New Testament: I am the way the truth and the life. I am Alpha, Omega, beginning and ending the first and the last, I am the one which was, which is and which is to come. I am Living Water, I am bread of life. I am truth. I am salvation. I am hope. I am the peace maker. I am the Christ, the Son of the Living God. I am the risen Savior. I am the only unique Son of God. I am the God of Abraham, Isaac and Jacob.

By God making this distinction, as to who He was, He was telling Moses you do not have to go to Egypt intimidated and shy. You do not have to be afraid. Moses you are being sent with the highest credentials. You are being sent by the highest power of the universe. Moses "I Am" has sent you.

God told Moses how he was to deal with Pharaoh. How he was to deal with Egypt, and how to deal with the Children of Israel. After all that Moses heard and had seen from God, he still needed more assurance from God. Fear became his closest companion. Moses **first fear** was he and his lack of being qualified for the task God was calling him to do. Moses **second fear**, was the fear of failure. Not being able to fulfill the task God called him to do. Moses **third fear** was the fear of rejection. After getting to Egypt, the people might not accept him as a God called leader.

Exodus 4:1 KJV,
*"And Moses answered and said,
But, behold, they will not believe me,
nor hearken unto my voice: for they will say,
The Lord hath not appeared unto thee."*

Exodus 4:10 KJV,
*"And Moses said unto the Lord, O my Lord,
I am not eloquent, neither heretofore,
nor since thou hast spoken unto thy servant:
but I am slow of speech, and of a slow tongue."*

The Lord began to deal directly with all these fears Moses was having. The Lord asked him a direct question, "What is that in your hand?" "This is a rod that I have in my hand." "Cast it down on the ground," the Lord told him. So Moses threw down the staff, and it turned into a snake! Moses jumped back. Then the Lord told Moses to reach out and grab its tail. So Moses reached out and grabbed it, and it turned back into a rod again in his hand.

The Lord told Moses to go and do these things that he had been shown so that they would believe he was sent by the God of their ancestors, the God of Abraham, the God of Isaac, and the God of Jacob. Then the Lord told Moses to put his hand into his bosom. Moses put his hand inside his cloak over his bosom, and when he took it out again, his hand was white as snow with leprosy. The Lord then told Moses to put his hand back into his bosom and when he had done this his hand was as healthy as the rest of his body. The Lord then told Moses if they are not convinced by either of these signs. Take some water from the Nile river and pour it out on the dry land and the water will become blood on the dry land. But with these three signs Moses was still not ready to go to Pharaoh and to bring the Children of Israel out.

Exodus 4:10 KJV,
"And Moses said unto the Lord, O my Lord,
I am not eloquent, neither heretofore,
nor since thou hast spoken unto thy servant:
but I am slow of speech, and of a slow tongue."

Moses was still trying to convince God he was not the right man. He was basically telling the Lord he was not good at speaking. He was telling the Lord he had never been good at speaking and surely I cannot go to Pharaoh and speak. I am so tongue-tied, and I get my words so tangled and twisted up. Then the Lord told Moses, "Who has made man's mouth? Who decides whether a person can speak or cannot speak, hear or cannot hear, see or cannot see? Is has always been me, the Lord. Now Moses I want you to go! I will be with you as you speak, and I will instruct you in what to say."

Notice that God did not at anytime tell Moses that he would have to be something he was not. Nor did God ever tell him he would have to use something he did not have. God will always use what you have. He will always let you be yourself. He will then use as you are as you develop into the disciplined individual He wants you to be. God can take the common things of life and use them in the supernatural. He can take the things that we call normal, you know the things that are natural and make it become divine and holy. Yes, with a little bit of nothing God can cause a miracle to happen. Moses rod, which was a common shepherd's rod, became a miracle rod when God touched it. Moses a man who was a tongue-tied and inhibited speaker, became the leader of the Children of Israel.

There is a reason that so many of us who call ourselves saints of God, Christians, never seem to make progress in our living for God. It is because we keep our eyes on our self. We look at the weaknesses of our own flesh. We are inhibited like Moses was. Yes, many of us have been told by others we cannot do it we never will be able to do anything and we have taken that into our spirit as the gospel truth. God calls you and tells you what He wants you to do and you say, *"Who Am I?"*

I do know what I am writing about here from a very personal point of view. I was seventeen years old when God began to deal with me and placed a call upon my life. I was not the best academic student that had ever been in the school system at Westlake High School. I had been told by many of my high school teachers and coaches, that I did not have it. I had taken two years of "Speech" classes both my teachers told me I did not have it, I would never ever be able to stand before a crowd of people and speak. I was a very timid and shy young man. I felt inferior to all of my peers. I knew my abilities were very limited. In 1966 after graduating from high School, I enrolled in Texas Bible College, located in Houston, Texas. I went over for my pre-registration and met some of the current students and faculty. My pastor at the time, said he did not like the young men in his church attending a Bible College, because they always ruined good young men. My father and mother, who were both highly educated wanted me to attend McNeese State in Lake Charles, Louisiana and get a secular degree, before I went for my degree from Bible College, because of accreditation. I then pulled my application for attending Texas Bible College and went and enrolled at McNeese State. I was never so out of place in all of my life. Needless to say I was a failure in my college career. I married on June 24, 1967 to the beautiful young lady that I had started dating my senior year in high school. Sandy is still my wife today and has been for over forty years. For the next twenty to twenty three years, I struggled in my walk with God, simply because I did not know who I was. I failed in every aspect of living. I failed in business endeavors. I failed as a father and a husband. I was a hard worker and I would do everything to give my wife and sons the best that I could. But I did not know how to really give them the thing they needed most and that was me. I lived frustrated and intimidated and most often I was a failure. I went to church most of the time. But as far as my relationship with the Lord it was up and down, like a yo-yo. Oh how I wish someone would have taught me some of these things when I was a younger man.

At the age of thirty, I and my family moved to Lake Charles, Louisiana for a short period of time. We started attending Apostolic Temple United Pentecostal Church on Holly Hill road. **Dr. Marvin Treece was our pastor.** *Next to the Lord Jesus Christ, this great pastor has been our salvation. If I can just be a small portion of the pastor, preacher that he was to us, I will feel I have been successful in my endeavor.* My family eventually moved out of Lake Charles to Buhler, Louisiana. This was some twenty or so miles from Apostolic Temple, but we continued to attend driving past many churches to get there.

At the age of forty years old, the Lord began to deal with me again about preaching His Word. I was on the backside of my desert at the time. My two sons were having major problems in their lives. I was struggling in my business dealings again. I had been teaching a Bible study in Mossville, Louisiana for almost nine years, this was a black community. These dear wonderful people came and told me they were not willing to continue in this study anymore, they were going back to where they were before. My wife had had some major surgery and was having so many struggles with the empty nest syndrome, because her sons left home at about the same time. My life was in shambles again. One day when I was on the floor in the living room of our home crying out to God. I had my face buried in the carpet and my tears were running like a free flowing spring.

God began to talk to my heart about preaching. I like Moses ask, **"God Who Am I**?" Lord you really do not understand, I can't go preach now, I am forty years old. I am no longer young and robust like I use to be. I am over-the-hill now Lord. I have bulges in my body, I don't have the stature or the looks to be a successful evangelist. Lord my body aches and I have never even so much as led a service in my life. Lord I do not know how to prepare a message and I sure do not have the abilities to deliver it if I had a message. So many excuses I gave Him that day.

I began to tell the Lord I would do anything that He wanted me to do. I instantly began to feel in my spirit the fact that He told me what to do twenty three years before. Until I did what He told me to then He had nothing else for me to do. I answered Him and said, "okay Lord, if this is what you want you are going to have to help me, but I am going to do it." I stopped making excuses. I got up off the floor, wiped my face and dried my tears and stopped crying. I went into the room where my wife was seated in a recliner and told her that I was going to change my profession. She ask what I would be selling now. I told her we were going to be traveling to all the beautiful mountainous states in this country. She again ask what I would be selling. I told her I was not selling anything, I was going to preach as a traveling evangelist. I went to my pastor and told him what my new plans were. This was in May of 1987, and the last week of June, my wife and I left our home in Buhler to preach the gospel.

I evangelized for almost thirteen years and have pastored two churches one in Georgia and now New Chapel Pentecostal Church in Collins, Mississippi. I have been preaching twenty years. I have preached in sixteen different states. I have been to the Yukon Territory to preach eight or nine times. I have preached in many of the churches in Alaska, having been in Alaska eleven different times. I have preached almost two thousand different messages, in more churches than I can count. I have preached in Pentecostal Churches, Baptist Churches, and Methodist Churches. I have preached in Camp Meetings across this country. I have seen hundreds of people filled with the Baptism of the Holy Ghost. I have seen hundreds baptized in Jesus Name, with me personally baptizing many of them. I have seen miracles, signs and wonders in these years of my ministry. I am still seeing God do exploits today.

I am so thankful that even when I did not know who I was, I knew who He was and was able to listen to His still small voice as He dealt with me. I am glad that He did not stop dealing with me because of my failures and inadequacies. I am glad He did not listen to all my excuses. I have learned so much over the past twenty years of my life, to God be the glory.

Philippians 4:12-13 KJV,
"I know both how to be abased, and I know
how to abound: everywhere and in all things
I am instructed both to be full and to be hungry,
both to abound and to suffer need.
I can do all things through Christ
which strengtheneth me."

Yes, all we can see is our preconceived weaknesses, our inadequacies, or timid, shy ways. God keeps telling us He is sending us and He is going to be there doing the work through us. We keep asking "**Who Am I?**" Why don't we all do ourselves a great big favor, get our eyes off ourselves, get ourselves out of the way and let God be the Deliverer and Savior of the world. All God needs today is simply common people, who have open hearts and are willing and obedient to His will and His purpose.

Moses went through preparation two thirds (2/3rd) of his entire life and was fulfilling God's will and purpose only one third (1/3rd) of his entire life.

Matthew 6:34 KJV,
*"Take therefore no thought for the morrow:
for the morrow shall take thought for the things
of itself. Sufficient unto the day is the evil thereof."*

CHAPTER FOUR

"Do Not Worry About Tomorrow"

This principle, I am writing about in this lesson. Is a principle that I have personally learned during some my hardest and most devastating times of my life.

Now I am of the opinion that everybody (Christian or non-Christian) will face some difficult times during their lifetime.

It is during these difficult dark, cruel times of our life that we learn endurance; that we muster up the strength and the courage to keep on keeping on.

I am reminded of a story I read some years back, in a Newspaper. A gentleman seemed to be looking for his place in life. With a backpack, strapped over his shoulders and an Alaskan malamute dog, he started to walk across America. For five years he spent walking across this nation. He went from the West Coast to the East Cost and back. Actually went thru a portion of all the lower 48 states, later to even tour Alaska. When he came to the end of his five year trip the news media met him in the State of Oregon. They ask him, "What the most difficult part of his trip, what one thing nearly made you give up and quit." He said, "I made it thru the desserts of Arizona and New Mexico, with seemingly no problems." "I made it thru the high rocky mountain climbs." "I made it thru the muggy weather in the south." He said he was beaten and robbed twice on this trip, didn't stop him. The changes in the weather and climate did not seem to affect him." He said, "I guess the most difficult thing I had to deal with on this entire trip, was the daily grind of sand that would get into my shoes. Yes, that is what it was, those tiny small grains of sand daily grinding in my shoes, almost made me quit.

I want to be very plain with you that are reading this manuscript. In most of our cases as human beings, it will not be the great big battles with sin that will defeat us in our walk with God. Yes, most of us that will take the time to read this manuscript will not struggle with booze or drugs. Nor, will the majority of us be caught up in what we call deep dark sin. But, what we do see defeating so many of our friends and relatives in this hour and day, is the everyday grind of life. Just the pressures of life cause us to quit, giving up and not living for God. The pressures of life are not sin, friend. But when we give in to them that will lead us into sin. These pressures of life will cause us to stay away from church and not live for God. Every one of us must shake ourselves, awaken ourselves to this problem, or the everyday grind of it all will break us down. It will defeat us, and totally destroy any hope of being with the Lord. These everyday pressures could be causing some to end up in hell.

I am trying to sound the warning through this writing. Even many of us who class ourselves as saints of God, had best be aware of these daily pressures of life; of the everyday grind of life. If we are not careful; those small grinds of life will defeat us.

Many of you may be thinking, while you are reading, "What are you talking about preacher?" "What are the grinds of life?" "What are the little things that might get in my way of living for God?"

I am talking about our daily living. I am talking about the old 9 to 5, 8 to 4, 7 to 3, JOB, whatever the hours are that you work your job. I am talking about making your pay-day, paying your bills, taking care of your automobiles; car wash, oil change, general maintenance and repairs, maintaining your home, inside and out, washing your dishes and your clothes, preparing your meals, hauling your children from one activity to another, cleaning your house. Mowing your grass, and so many other things you do to live a day of your life.

If you and I are going to be successful in both life and living for God, we are going to have to learn the secret of living for God right in the middle of the everyday grind of life. If we do not learn this secret, the everyday grind is going to burn us out. If we do not learn this secret, the everyday grind of life will defeat us and soon conquer our chances of ever living for God.

We can try if we want to, but we will never get away from life. There will always be those grinding, nagging things we must face every day.

Life is a dictator! There is a job we must go to. There are bills that we must pay. We have obligations to take care of, like a spouse and children. There are thing that we must take care of day in and day out.

We face the daily grind on our job. We face the daily grind in our town. We face the daily grinds around our house, even in our house. Yes we face the grinds of our home.

The daily grind often starts when the alarm fails to go off in the morning. Therefore we are now late for work. The house payment is overdue. The electricity is due to be turned off today. The car is broke down. The baby is sick and needing medicine. My aunt Suzy is sick and in the hospital. My uncle Frank is in the morgue. Washing machine is broke down. Sewer is stopped up. Yard needs mowing. Children are rebelling. Spouse is yelling. Neighbors won't speak. The preacher announces revival every night this week.

Friend this is life. Every day there is going to be that nagging, that pressing, hurting grind that we must face. When we really get to thinking about life. We look at those who come to church with us, they are always so bubbly with happiness and joy. Many of us observe this with questions in our mind. "Why don't they have to live like I do?" "Why is life so easy for them?" "Why don't they have to face the grind like I do?"

But when we really step back and take a deep look at their lives, you know when we investigate them. We find they have to live this life also. Every day they face their same old hurtful grind. Our obligations and responsibilities may all be somewhat different. Our lives are all somewhat different but, we all face our grinds of life.

What we must do in this hour, is to stop feeling sorry for ourselves. Stop comparing ourselves with each other. Learn how to live for God in the midst of life and in spite of this daily grind.

I hear people talking and asking questions of one another all the time. "Why does God allow all of this pressure in my life?" "Why does He allow all of these troubles?"

Does the Lord not even care? I am a Holy Ghost filled Child of God, I don't deserve all of this."

Job 14:1 KJV,
"Man that is born of a woman is of few days, and full of trouble."

Proverbs 17:17 (b) KJV,
"...and a brother is born for adversity."

Psalms 34:19 KJV,
"Many are the afflictions of the righteous: but the Lord delivereth him out of them all."

According to Job our lives will be short and full of trouble. Proverbs tells us we are born for adversity. In the Psalms we find that even the righteous will face many afflictions.

Writer's note:
"The word afflictions did not seem serious when I first read it in this scripture. It was something so simple: like a burr under a horse's blanket.

In the dictionary I found something quite amazing:
Afflictions ~ *"Adversities, calamities, distresses, evils, harms, heaviness, troubles, wrongs, sorrows, hurts, etc, etc,"*

It does not matter who you are, you were born into this life, this living, and therefore you were born into this everyday grind!

I do not want to sound negative in my writings. Nor do I want to burst some of your little angelic spiritual bubbles. But as long as you and I are on the face of this green earth, the grind of life is not going to get better.

We are living in the last days. Perilous times are upon us! The pressures of life are going to get tougher. The grind of life is going to be rough. The only ones who are going to overcome, are those who have their minds made up, those who are sold out to God, those who are watching and praying, who are faithful, and who are working for God in spite of the grind.

Think about this. Every day you hear of so many changes going on around us. Companies are being bought in mergers or companies going out of business. Thousands of people are being laid off. People having to change careers and find a new source of income. The bills do not stop when the job stops, they keep coming. That does not stop the car from breaking down and needing costly repairs. That does not stop the children from getting sick and needing medical attention or medication. That does not stop the electric bill, water bills and telephone bills. That does not stop the need for buying groceries. As long as you and I are on the face of this earth, we will awaken every morning to face the daily grind. Jesus told His disciples, (let me paraphrase in my words),

Matthew 6:34 (a),
*"Don't worry about tomorrow;
let tomorrow take care of itself..."*

Now if the cares and struggles of life are going to always be with us. We then are going to have to learn how to live for God in the midst of them. We are going to have to learn how to live and exist among all the things that life brings our way. We are going to have o learn to endure, to overcome and survive. The Apostle Paul wrote to Timothy:

2 Timothy 4:5 KJV,
*"But watch thou in all things,
endure afflictions, do the work of an evangelist,
make full proof of thy ministry."*

Paul is simply telling Timothy to be spiritual awake, attentive and alert at all times. Bear up under the pain and fatigue of life. Tolerate and put up with the old grind of life itself. Do not flinch, Timothy, do not give Satan one inch. Actively teach, preach and witness and win souls for the kingdom of God. Prove to the world and Satan you really are called and chosen by God.

Every one of you that read this manuscript, have your own cares and pressures of life. You have your own struggles and burdens. Your grind of life is not just like mine and my grind of life is not just like yours. We each carry a different load as we journey through life each day.

I have personally come to the realization we as Christians cannot get weary with life. We cannot throw our hands up and quit. We cannot give up. Paul told Timothy, "in the last days it is going to be difficult to live for God, because even the people of God will cave in under the pressures of life."

The reason there is such a rise in suicide is because people from every walk of life are caving under the cares of life. They get so weary and are weighted down by the everyday grind of life. We must understand the Word of God gives us fair warning about all of this.

Galatians 6:9 KJV,
"And let us not be weary in well doing:
for in due season we shall reap, if we faint not."

I can promise you that some of you who are reading this manuscript, are weary. Circumstances of your life have pressed against you. People have turned on you and said all types of things against you. The grind of all this has put much pressure on you. You are really weary under this weight.

If you are not weary at this moment, count your blessings, because somewhere in your life you will become weary. You must understand, because we are all human, we are all born into the grind of this world. There are certain responsibilities and pressures of life that we will all face. I would like to challenge each of you, DO NOT GIVE UP! DO NOT QUIT!

When we read through the Bible, we see so many hero's of faith. We feel that these great men and women were super humans. They seemingly could overcome anything that came against them. We feel that the pressures of life never affected them. To this I say "Hog Wash!" These people had to face the old grind just like we do. Many times the pressures and the grinding weighted on them just like it does on us today.

2 Corinthians 1:8 KJV,
"For we would not, brethren, have you ignorant of our trouble which came to us in Asia, that we were pressed out of measure, above strength, insomuch that we despaired even of life:"

2 Corinthians 4:8-9 KJV,
"We are troubled on every side, yet not distressed; we are perplexed, but not in despair; Persecuted, but not forsaken; cast down, but not destroyed;"

The Apostle Paul faced the grind of life with assurance.

2 Corinthians 5:7 KJV,
"(For we walk by faith, not by sight) ☺*"*

Philippians 4:13 KJV,
"I can do all things through Christ which strengtheneth me."

Too many Christians live for God by feelings alone. If you are one that is living for God by feelings and not by faith, the devil has you so confused and messed up; he keeps your life in shambles. We who are saints of God can do all things through Jesus Christ. He is our strength and our sustainer.

I want to plead with you not to become weary with life. Do not become over-whelmed by life. Do not become depressed because of life. By all means do not give up on life. It is not the will of God for His people to be defeated by life. Jesus gave His life on the old rugged cross. He shed His precious blood so that humanity could be set free. Jesus paid for our redemption and provided us with liberty. He is our provider of peace, love, joy and salvation. He has provided us a way of escape from the pressures of this life. We must take advantage of the provisions provided by Jesus Christ our Lord and Savior.

Philippians 4:6-7 KJV,
"Be careful for nothing; but in every thing by prayer and supplication with thanksgiving let your requests be made known unto God.

And the peace of God, which passeth all understanding, shall keep your hearts and minds through Christ Jesus."

Paul is simply telling the Philippians, *"Don't worry, be happy! Live by faith and trust in the Lord."*

I was so weary and tired after a flight from Lake Charles, Louisiana by way of Houston, Texas landed in Anchorage, Alaska. This was a flight that normally took about thirteen hours of time, including two layovers. This particular time we had several delays and flight changes so it was about twenty one hours. The plane taxied down the runway and slowly pulled up to the terminal gate. The engines shut down and they told us we could get off the plane. I took my carry on and my brief case, strolled down the aisle and into the airport terminal. My head was pounding, my ears needed to pop, and I could not hear well. I saw Brother Ron Herring and Brother Client Playle, two great men that I have known for fifteen years or more. We smiled, shook hands, hugged necks and exchanged hello's and started walking to the baggage claims area. Brother Playle said to me, "well how was your flight and how are you doing, Brother Bankens?" I do not think either of these men was ready for my response. I answered something like this, *"How am I doing, ha, ha; I am simply letting life unfold."*

I could tell by the puzzled looks on both their faces, that they had not been ready for that answer. By nature I am usually a positive and upbeat person. I have been a motivator and promoter all of my adult life. I usually respond to a question of this nature with, "I am doing great," "fantastic," "terrific." I have always been one that had been a positive, upbeat, and motivated, you know everything is terrific kind of guy. But I had had a rough twenty one hours on planes, in air port terminals, with no rest and very little to eat. Life had been a grind that day.

Here is the truth of the matter. I am not always on the top of the world. I am not always feeling terrific or great. Sometimes life is a pressure cooker. Sometimes I am right in the middle of a battle. Sometimes I wake up in the morning feeling down, sick or afflicted. Sometimes life is caving in from all sides and I cannot seem to change the circumstances I am facing. Yes, sometimes life is just a hard grind.

I have learned that I do not have to fake my way through the difficult times and situations. To be a Christian, does not require me to have a man made artificial positive attitude. At the same time I have learned that I cannot walk around feeling sorry for myself. Neither can I continually share my doom, gloom and despair with others. I must take life as it comes my way. I must live every day to the best of my abilities. I must not let the grind of this life make me sit down and give up. I must simply let life unfold as it wills and thank God for being with me and helping me through each and every day.

Not one of us is in control of life. Neither can any of us predict tomorrow. But we all can trust God who is the giver of life and the one that controls tomorrow.

Years ago when I was a fifteen year old high school student, I was having some difficulties with my academics at school. My parents knew that I was struggling, they really wanted things to be better for me. All I could talk about at that time was, "*I could not wait until I could get away from that old grind.*" I even let it be known that I would be sixteen in a couple months and I was going to quit school. My teachers did not really seem to care, it would just be one less problem for them. My parents would threaten me and tell me I better get that foolish idea out of my head. But I had enough the grind was more than I seemingly could handle.

My old grandfather, Johnnie M. Banken, Sr., who had less than a fourth grade education, knew I was in a dilemma. One afternoon after he and I had worked in his field, we were sitting in the breeze way of his little home. He began to talk to me about life, and about the struggles of living. He told me there were things that I did not understand or even comprehend at this time. You must take life as it comes to you. You cannot give up every time life does not suit you. You just hang in there, it will get better.

My grandfather got up out of his rocking chair walked over to the side of the house. There he pulled out his pocket knife and cut a beautiful, rose bud off the rose bush. He walked back over to where I sat and gave me the rose bud. He said, "I want you to pull each petal on this rose bud into the position that will make it a beautiful rose." As I began to pull these petals into position, they began to break and fall off the rose bud. When I finished pulling the last petal, I had an awful mess. All I had left in my hand was the stubble of the bud, with the petals laying everywhere.

Sufficient Grace when Your Life is in the Sewer

My grandfather began to speak some wisdom into me. You are like this rose bud son. You are out there on a limb all by yourself. The elements of life will hammer you and the storms will come and go. The sun will beat on you day in and day out. But if you will hang on to the stem, never take yourself from the bush, hang on to the vine son, you will survive. Just as life comes against you, let it unfold. Like the rosebud, off the rose bush, you must unfold as life allows and you will eventually bloom into a beautiful rose. When your time comes our heavenly Father will pick that rose and add it to his heavenly bouquet.

Many years have passed since my grandfather gave me that great lesson. I personally laid that little lesson aside for much of my life. I got so wrapped up with being successful that I began to follow the thoughts and lessons of many motivators and promoters. "Fake it till you make it," and "If you are having difficulties or problems you have no faith." Both of these ideas are pure "Hog Wash." We must live life as it comes to us. Yes, I must change the things that I can change to make my circumstances better, but there are so many things that I cannot change. My attitude does need to stay upbeat and positive. My disposition should always be kind, gentle and sweet. I must stop worrying and fretting and be happy as I am. I must also understand, under no circumstances can I even consider giving up or quitting. I cannot get angry at God or anyone else and quit. I must face my daily grind as it comes and simply let it unfold.

Growing and learning, that is what the Christian life is in a nutshell. You and I as saints of God will have more growing and learning days in life than we do great, fantastic or terrific days. This world that we live in is a world that grinds.

The world view teaches us different lessons than the Word of God does. They teach that you can think your way out of the grind of life. Think yourself positive, thing and grow rich. They teach us to speak ourselves positive, talk ourselves into happiness and talk ourselves into success. But life itself teaches us that for us to grow properly there are lessons that we must learn and difficulties that we must face. To learn, we must have our own experiences. We must face the grind of life our self. We must cross every obstacle in life and endure each and every circumstance that comes to us. Only then will we make it as over-comers.

The experiences that we go through and the lessons of life are not always pleasant. These are not always good things or good times to remember. Sometimes these experiences are very rough and painful. Sometimes they are times of endurance, which are often slow and difficult. Many times these experiences are just downright awful; so bad you do not want to talk about them.

Often in the grind of life, we take three steps forward and we get knocked back six or seven steps. We must always remember, it does not matter where life brings us or how difficult today seems; Jesus Christ is still Lord. He is still a good God and the victory is still ours if we will just hang in there until the end.

Life is not a "Six-Flag" vacation. It is not an every day party. It is not a time when everything will be picture perfect and good. Jesus did not say come follow me and I will give you a balanced check book every morning. No, you have to personally keep it balanced. He did not promise anyone of us that life would be a rose garden. Such expectations from the Lord are so unrealistic. The Lord did not guarantee His followers a life of ease. But He does let us know that we can all be a rose in His garden, if we will hang on the vine and simply let life unfold.

Lessons in life come to us in many different forms. But, there are times that we are going through the grind of life that we wonder if we can handle any more lessons at all.

The late seventies into the early eighties, I will never forget the lessons I learned then. My children had both been afflicted and were in and out of the hospitals so many times. My wife was a continual nurse maid to them. I was in the "Cement Finishing" business. To be very honest with you, I loved finishing cement over any other job that I have ever done. The work was back breaking hard, but the finished product was something to look at and be proud of. Over a four year period I was involved in so many finishing jobs in the Westlake, Lake Charles and Sulphur, Louisiana areas. I can go back in that area even today and see homes, buildings, roads and parking lots that I poured back then that still look good.

I had never dreamed of being a "Cement Finisher" and had no idea how it was done. It was during the time I was Mr. Rooter that Leon came to me and told me he was struggling and needed some help. He made me a business proposition, if I would buy the tools that we needed, he would teach me how to be a great finisher. I must confess the first few days that I was out there in the heat of the summer, I really thought I had lost my mind. I would go home at night so tired, my feet, legs, hand, arms and back would just ache with such excruciating pain. I would get up the next day and go work in that heat again.

I was still in a financial bind from the down turn I took in 1978 and I only had one automobile, it was a 1977 Cadillac Deville. We would put the big toweling machine, bull float, jitter bug and all the hand tools in the trunk of the car. We would drive up to the job and people would be utterly amazed.

Leon and I had this deal going. If we were going to one of his customers to bid a job, I would put on a little chauffer cap and drive him up to the job. I would get out and place a red carpet on the ground for him to get out on and he would go bid the job. If it was my customer He wore the hat and chauffeured me. Oh, what good memories those are. The reason that this has any significance at all is that Leon was a stocky, but small in stature, short black man and I was a tall, large white man. People could not get over the fact we worked so good and so close together.

I was teaching Bible study at Sister Moriah Miles, home every Monday night in those days. There were many of the men that attended that Monday night Bible study worked with Leon and I, pouring and finishing cement. One particular Monday night we were in study and this scripture was read:

Romans 8:28k KJV,
"And we know that all things work together for good to them that love God, to them who are the called according to his purpose."

Jack spoke up and said to me, "my dear brother, how can you hang on to that scripture?" He went on to say, "there is no possible way this scripture can be from God. There is nothing good working for you right now and there sure isn't anything working good for me." He said, look at us, we say we are Christians and we trust God, but we wake up every morning and we go out in the hot sun and we pull concrete and we then finish it, our backs are breaking, show me the good."

I began to explain this scripture to him like this. This scripture does not say all things are good. It says all things work together for the good to them that love God and are called according to His purpose. He said, "my dear brother, you are going to have to do some better explaining than that." I told him that I would in our next Bible study.

I left there that night somewhat puzzled within myself, how was I going to explain that scripture in such a way he could see what it really means. I went home that night and went to sleep. In my sleep, I began to dream of my old grandmother in her kitchen on a cold winter morning. The gas stove was on she was getting breakfast ready for my grandfather and several of her grandsons that were there. In my dream I began to see how I was going to explain that scripture.

The next Monday night I arrived at Sister Moriah Miles home a few minutes early. I ask her to turn her oven to preheat about 400 degrees I had something I wanted to bake to illustrate Romans 8:28 in our Bible study. Once everyone was there I began my demonstration. I had plain flour, sugar, baking powder, salt, shortening and butter milk. I ask Jack to come help me. I told the group that each of these ingredients were not really good all by themselves. I got Jack to taste the flour, sugar, baking powder, salt, shortening and ever the butter milk. I ask him if any one of those ingredients were good to eat by themselves. His answer was no. He said that he could not make a meal out of any one of those ingredients. I mixed all of my dry ingredients together. I then mixed my shortening and butter milk together until blended. I began to slowly mix the dry mix into the liquid. I then rolled and mixed into a very stiff yet pliable consistency. I had two big cast iron skillets heating on the top of the stove and we cut the biscuits with a cup and place them into the preheated oven about thirty minutes. When they were browned and done, we all passed the biscuits the pure sugar cane syrup and had a wonderful time. When it was over I ask Jack, "if he understood Romans 8:28 a little better now." He said, "for the first time in my life, I understand that all things, whether good or bad, like the ingredients in the biscuits, are working together for my good, because I love God and am called by Him and I also understand these things work together to fulfill His purpose."

We must all realize this world that we live in will grind at us every single day. But we who place our trust in the Lord and serve Him with all of our heart know that everything is going to work together for the good as long as we stay in His will and fulfill His purpose.

If you are having a bad time in your life and do not know what to do, just hang in there. If life is grinding at you and you don't see any change in sight, just let life unfold as it will. Remember, you must live life one day at a time. Jesus Christ told His disciples, *"Don't worry about tomorrow, let tomorrow take care of itself."*

James 4:14 KJV,
"Whereas ye know not what shall be on the morrow.
For what is your life? It is even a vapour,
that appeareth for a little time,
and then vanisheth away."

Romans 11:33-36 KJV,
"O the depth of the riches both of the wisdom and knowledge of God! how unsearchable are his judgments, and his ways past finding out! For who hath known the mind of the Lord? or who hath been his counsellor? Or who hath first given to him, and it shall be recompensed unto him again? For of him, and through him, and to him, are all things: to whom be glory for ever. Amen."

CHAPTER FIVE

"Lord I Still Trust You!"

(The McFalls, from Meridian, Mississippi sang a song several years ago. The title was, "I Still Trust You Lord." When I heard them sing that in concert one night, I went to my travel trailer and wrote the notes to the message of which this chapter was taken, that was in 1994. I have preached it all over the USA, even into Alaska and Canada.)

Sufficient Grace when Your Life is in the Sewer

When our lives are young and our health is good, we view life with so much hope. We live with so much vigor and vitality. We are just carefree and happy as the good times roll past us so very fast.

There comes that time in every one's life, that we must face some difficult circumstances. You know those times of disappointments, those times of sickness and even disease, those times of so much sorrow and pain. Those times when the pieces of life's puzzle just refuses to fit. I am talking about those times when the God of love; the God that you have served all these years is simply not making any sense in your life.

It is in the midst of times like this, when we are so tangled up in confusions. We are mixed up in the crises of our lives. We begin to question our walk with God. We begin to ask God, *"Why, God?" "Why are you allowing this to happen to me and my family?"*

When you and I are so wrapped up in the different crises of our lives? It is common for humans to question. It is common for us to be frustrated, even with God. It is our feeble human inabilities to figure out what God is doing in all of this, that cause us our greatest problems. This in turn causes us to question God and to question ourselves.

John the Baptist, who was the forerunner of Jesus Christ, the one that had made the statement, "he was unworthy to even stoop and loosen the sandals on Jesus feet." The one that baptized Jesus in the Jordan River and saw the Spirit of the Lord descend from heaven as a dove and light on Jesus. Also, he was the one that heard the voice of the Lord say, "This is my beloved Son in whom I am well pleased." When John was placed in prison, he sent two of his disciples to Jesus to question.

Matthew 11:3 KJV,
"And said unto him, Art thou he that should come, or do we look for another?"

Even the greatest of Christians have questioned in their lifetime. Even the greatest saints of God have shown their humanity in the midst of life's turmoil's and crises.

Throughout the Book of Psalms, we have seen the psalmist's question "Why?"

Psalms 22:1-2 KJV, A Psalm of David.
"My God, my God, why hast thou forsaken me? why art thou so far from helping me, and from the words of my roaring? O my God, I cry in the daytime, but thou hearest not; and in the night season, and am not silent."

Even when Jesus Christ was on the cross of Calvary, humanity questioned "Why?"

Matthew 27:46 KJV,
"And about the ninth hour Jesus cried with a loud voice, saying, Eli, Eli, lama sabachthani? that is to say, My God, my God, why hast thou forsaken me?"

Yes, most often when we find ourselves in any crises, we humans question "Why?" Most often, this question will go unanswered. For years and even for our entire lifetime, we may never know the answers to these questions.

As Christians we had best be braced and prepared for these times. Whether we like to admit it or not, we are all going to walk through these places that cause us to question.

Psalms 34:19 KJV,
*"Many are the afflictions of the righteous:
but the Lord delivereth him out of them all."*

The sad thing that I see in all of this as a pastor, there are so many saints of God, church going Christians, who are shaken at these points of their life. They feel that God has abandoned them. They then throw up their hands and say, "what's the use?"

This is Satan's tactic on you and me. He wants us to feel that our compassionate Lord and Savior has singled us out for abuse. We must understand, as human beings we do not think, comprehend or act as God does.

Isaiah 55:8-9 KJV,
*"For my thoughts are not your thoughts,
neither are your ways my ways, saith the Lord.
For as the heavens are higher than the earth,
so are my ways higher than your ways,
and my thoughts than your thoughts."*

When it seems like God is not making any sense in your life. Do not become disillusioned or fall into the depths of despair. Do not give up! Do not quit!

Psalms 34:17-18 KJV,
"The righteous cry, and the Lord heareth, and delivereth them out of all their troubles. The Lord is nigh unto them that are of a broken heart; and saveth such as be of a contrite spirit."

The psalmists lets us know that that the Lord hears the cries of all His people and will deliver them out of their troubles. The Lord is very close to you when you have a broken heart and will save all who are sorry for their sins. When you are in the valley and you think you are all alone in this place of sorrow and despair. Just stop for a moment and look around you. You will see multitudes of hurting people who are in that same valley with you. You are not the only one with problems. You are not the only one with aches, hurts and pains. You are not the only one with tragedy.

Matthew 5:45 (b) KJV,
"...for he maketh his sun to rise on the evil and on the good, and sendeth rain on the just and on the unjust."

Peter said it so well in the household of Cornelius.

Acts 10:34 KJV,
"Then Peter opened his mouth, and said, Of a truth I perceive that God is no respecter of persons:"

None of us are the first human being to suffer.

1 Peter 2:21 KJV,
"For even hereunto were ye called: because Christ also suffered for us, leaving us an example, that ye should follow his steps:"

Neither are we the first or the only saint of God to suffer.

1 Peter 5:8-11 KJV,
"Be sober, be vigilant; because your adversary the devil, as a roaring lion, walketh about, seeking whom he may devour: Whom resist stedfast in the faith, knowing that the same afflictions are accomplished in your brethren that are in the world. But the God of all grace, who hath called us unto his eternal glory by Christ Jesus, after that ye have suffered a while, make you perfect, stablish, strengthen, settle you. To him be glory and dominion for ever and ever. Amen."

If we could ever get it in our mindset that people everywhere are struggling. People from every facet of society, every race, creed, color and culture have afflictions in their life.

Job 14:1-2 KJV,
"Man that is born of a woman is of few days, and full of trouble.

*He cometh forth like a flower, and is cut down:
he fleeth also as a shadow, and continueth not."*

James 4:14 KJV,
*"Whereas ye know not what shall be on the morrow.
For what is your life? It is even a vapour,
that appeareth for a little time, and then
vanisheth away."*

We as human beings do not have all of the answers. Neither will we ever understand all that happens in our lifetime. But this one thing we do know, if we are truly filled with His Spirit. In our good times and our bad times, our faith, trust and hope should be in Jesus Christ and nothing less. Where ever we find ourselves in life we must be able to say with assurance, "Yes, Lord I still trust you."

We know beyond a shadow of a doubt, that good, godly, righteous, Holy Ghost filled people will suffer many afflictions. We also know that the ungodly, evil, bad people will suffer many afflictions.

Psalms 34:19-22 KJV,
*"Many are the afflictions of the righteous:
but the Lord delivereth him out of them all.
He keepeth all his bones: not one of them is broken.
Evil shall slay the wicked: and they that hate
the righteous shall be desolate.
The Lord redeemeth the soul of his servants: and
none of them that trust in him shall be desolate."*

I will never forget the many tragedies that have come to my family, especially when my two sons, Robbie and Kevin were younger. My eldest son, Robbie, fell and broke his right hip socket in August of 1981. He was thirteen years old at the time. He has had three major hip surgeries which left his right leg 2 ¼ inches shorter than his left leg. He will live with this the rest of his life. My youngest son, Kevin, had his left eye put out in December 1981, at the annual Christmas fireworks display in Natchitoches, Louisiana. He was twelve years old at the time. He also will live with his injury the rest of his life. Both of my sons were injured a few months apart in the same year. None of this made sense to me then and I still cannot make sense of it. But through it all my wife and I never blamed God, we still trusted God through this.

In March 1982 my dad was diagnosed with stomach cancer and went through two surgeries and several rounds of chemotherapy treatments. My dad was a great saint of God and a man with much faith. I watched him as he lived that next seventeen and one half months with dignity. My dad never seemed to question God. He did not use his illness as a reason to miss church, he was there every service except when he was in the hospital. The Saturday night before he passed away, he was in revival service and I went to be with him. After the service had ended he went into his office and made the church deposit, paid the few church bills that were due, and did the book work that he would normally do. I told him to just leave the work until the next day and he could do it when he returned to church the next morning. He looked at me and said, I won't be here in the morning. I just thought he was tired and feeling weak and did not feel that he would have the strength to be there the next day. But to my amazement my dad was up making preparations to get ready to go to Sunday morning service at church when he passed away. My dad passed away on Sunday morning, September 25, 1983.

My dad, Johnnie Matthew Bankens, Jr. left this world in victory, never blaming God. But I must confess this did not make sense to me. I could not understand it; my dad loved God, his church, his family, his pastor, all the saints of God in the church. My dad helped people from every walk of life, he worked hard to see people converted and saved from their life of sin. Even though I did not understand all that was happening, and it did not make any sense to me. I knew that God was in control, and I still trusted Him.

The great Apostle Paul suffered so much in this life. He was ostracized and ridiculed. He was beaten and jailed. Never blamed God or charged God foolishly, but simply trusted God through ever situation.

Philippians 1:20-21, Paul's Life for Christ,
New Living Translation ®,
"For I fully expect and hope that I will never be ashamed, but that I will continue to be bold for Christ, as I have been in the past.
And I trust that my life will bring honor to Christ, whether I live or die.

> *For to me, living means living for Christ, and dying is even better."*

Thanks be to our God and Savior Jesus Christ, the righteous have hope beyond this life. If we trust in Him we shall not be desolate, He will take care of our situations. "Lord, I still trust you!"

Saints of God, it is time that we wake up and realize, everyone suffers. But not all that suffer in this life will be saved.

Matthew 10:22 (b) KJV,
"…but he that endureth to the end shall be saved."

I guess one of the saddest things I have noticed in my ministry. There are so many saints of God who do not understand life. They do not get it, there are times in our lives when things do not add up at all. Our life has taken a turn for the worse, thing are terrible. Circumstances are bad and God seemingly is not making any sense. We become confused and disoriented with all that is now taking place. We feel like God has abandoned us out here to simply be defeated and die. No, God has not left you, He is right there with you in the middle of your travesty of life.

We have so many Christians who have bought into the message that God has a perfect plan of prosperity, health and happiness for those who are full of His Spirit. I will agree that God does have a perfect plan for all of those that serve Him. But that plan does not guarantee us a perfect life of tranquility, happiness and paradise on this earth. God does not even guarantee any perfection and tranquility while we live on this earth. God does not even guarantee we the saints of God health, wealth or happiness while we are serving Him.

For some the wonderful plan that God has for their life leaves them on a cane, on crutches or in a wheel chair the rest of their life. For some God's perfect plan leaves those with no sight, deafness and some cannot speak the rest of their lives. For some they will die young. For some it is a life of poverty. For some every day of living is a struggle.

> Philippians 1:29 New Living Translation ®,
> *"For you have been given not only the privilege of trusting in Christ but also the privilege of suffering for him."*

> 2 Timothy 2:12 KJV,
> *"If we suffer, we shall also reign with him: if we deny him, he also will deny us:"*

For the prophet Jeremiah the wonderful plan God had for his life found him in a dungeon, a dark murky pit. For the Apostles of the New Testament the wonderful plan of God for them, meant much outward abuse and persecution. Most of them faced a very horrible and terrible death. For you and I as saints of God today, God's plan is a wonderful and perfect plan. It will not be a rose garden picnic. It will not be a guarantee of ease and pleasure. But God's wonderful plan for our lives will land us safe home in heaven, if we are willing to fulfill God's will and purpose now.

Romans 8:28 KJV,
"And we know that all things work together for good to them that love God, to them who are the called according to his purpose."

God has a purpose for each one of us to fulfill. As long as we work for that end, we are in His will, and we will see everything working together for good. It is tragic when a saint of God sees little to no meaning in their life. On top of that they feel that God has forgotten them in the midst of their circumstances. These individuals have this feeling, that as long as things are good in their life, God loves them and is with them. But the moment they begin to have the slightest problem, and it is not immediately resolved by God the way they felt it should have been, God no longer loves them or cares for them. They then get down trodden and weary with distress. They become filled with anger and much depression. They express their bitterness and show their agitation openly. All the while they openly blame God.

There is no greater stress on us as human beings, than to build one's life on ideas and philosophies that do not line up with the Word of God, then to see all of this collapse around us. This just brings more stress and pain and adds to the troubles that are already accumulating. A Christian who is not anchored on the Word of God, who does not understand life and its struggles will become shaken.

There will be times in our walk with God that God will be silent. It will seem as though God is not even hearing our prayers. The heavens are closed and seem to be brazened like brass. As a child of God we will then feel all alone.

Job 1:1 KJV,
"There was a man in the land of Uz, whose name was Job; and that man was perfect and upright, and one that feared God, and eschewed evil."

Here we find a man that loved God with all his heart. This man was holy, righteous the scripture calls him perfect. He stayed away from evil, in fact he despised anything evil. This does not seem like a man that would be a candidate for disaster. According to modern day preachers and prophets this man should have been on easy street for the rest of his life. Yet we find this perfect, righteous man suffered staggering losses. Within just a few hours he lost his wealth, possessions, herds, children, servants, health, friends and his own reputation. But with all these loses and these tragedies, Job tore his clothing off, shaved his head then fell on the ground and worshipped God.

Job 1:21-22 KJV,
"And said, Naked came I out of my mother's womb, and naked shall I return thither: the Lord gave, and the Lord hath taken away; blessed be the name of the Lord. In all this Job sinned not, nor charged God foolishly."

We can only imagine how it was. Here was Job a saint of God, losing everything, worshipping God through all of this loss, sorrow and pain. God never even acted as though He heard job's cry, and God acted as though He really did not care. The reason I have come to that conclusion is God gave Satan permission to go after Job again. This time Job had boils on his head, feet, seat, arms, hands and body. Job has boils between his toes, up his nose he was a bloody mess of corruption. No comfort could he find. So on an ash heap, with a broken piece of pottery Job scrapes these boils on his body. As though this perfect and upright man did not have enough problems. His wife comes over and tells him to stop being so foolish, why don't you just give up go ahead and curse God so he will take you out of this miserable state and let you die. At this point most of us want to get really upset at "Sister Job." But let's think about her situation also. She was going through as much distress as was Job. She had lost her children, her home and possessions also. She was no longer married to the wealthiest man, but her husband the man she loved, was now in poverty, with boils all over his body and sitting at the city dump scrapping his wounds. All she could see was the doom, gloom, despair and agony.

I see Christian people in this day and hour give up and quit. Who have much less pain and struggle than she was encountering. We need to beware saints of God.

Job was still the head of his house, even in this condition. He told his wife she was speaking like a foolish woman, or a woman that had no faith.

Job 2:10 KJV,
"But he said unto her, Thou speakest as one of the foolish women speaketh. What? shall we receive good at the hand of God, and shall we not receive evil? In all this did not Job sin with his lips."

What an incredible man of faith. Nothing was going to separate him from the love of his God. He had his mind made up he had made a dedicated commitment to himself and to God. Yes, Job was still trusting God through all of this. I am totally convinced that God has given us plenty biblical examples that trusted Him in spite of their situation or conditions. But we can also look around the church and find so many daily examples of faith and trust in the Lord.

I have a friend who pastors a Baptist Church in Georgia. His name is Brother Gary Studdard. I have kept in touch with him since I left Georgia three years ago. He has gone through cancer surgery and many bouts of chemotherapy and has trusted God through it. I had him come preach for us since. He is just so upbeat with faith and trust in God.

I pastored a wonderful couple while I was in Georgia, Jimmie and Eva Walker. Sister Eva was diagnosed with cancer, as we were leaving Georgia and coming to Mississippi. Because of the circumstances, I told the new pastor at the church that I had just left that my wife and I were going to keep in touch with Sister Eva until she won the battle with cancer. She is so positive and upbeat,

Sister Eva is still trusting God on the other side of these hard and horrible treatments.

Sufficient Grace when Your Life is in the Sewer

In the church that I now pastor, I have had so many that have been ill, that have trusted God in spite of their sicknesses and diseases. Sister Mary Deen is one that has recently fought a battle with cancer and is winning that battle. Her faith in the midst of this battle has been so very strong. I have never heard a negative word from her. Her testimony has been if this is the course that the Lord has chosen for her life, she has enough faith in Him that she will trust Him all the way through this life to the end.

Brother Sam Bates has been a testimony to us all. One of the greatest men I have ever had the privilege of pastoring. He was diagnosed with a brain tumor, had the surgery in Hattiesburg, Mississippi. He then chose to have his treatments at M.D. Anderson in Houston, Texas. This man went to the door of death and has now come full circle to work full time on his job as an engineer. Brother Bates will tell you today, he still trust God.

Sister Rachael Burrell has had a bought with a disease that attacked her skin shortly after Hurricane Katrina hit the state of Mississippi in August of 2005. She has been to doctors of all types and specialties to see if they could diagnose her illness. The problem that she first fought on her skin is now inside her body attacking different organs. She is on Oxygen, almost full time now. She has had to miss church many times. But I go pray for her, and her faith is still strong. She still trusts the Lord to bring her all the way through.

Brother Matt Miller is a young man with a young family that was working a good job as a welder before I moved to Mississippi. He dropped a piece of heavy plate metal on his foot and broke it. During the healing of his foot he began to have excruciating pain in his foot and leg. This pain was so tremendous that he could not stand it. He has been diagnosed with the incurable disease called RSD. Brother Matt has to wear a brace on his leg at all times. Has a stimulator which goes directly to the nerves that go to his legs and feet, to send a shock wave when his pain gets so tremendous. He walks with a cane. He cannot climb stairs, because he falls really easy. He cannot hunt, fish or camp with his family. He cannot throw the ball with his son. He cannot run and play games with his two young children. But through all that he is going through, he is faithful to church, Bible Study, prayer meetings, church fellowships and so much more. His faith has never wavered. He does not understand his situation and does not like this situation he is in. But as he walks through all of this his faith is still strong and he is still trusting God.

When we as saints of God are permitted to go through emotional valleys, or spiritual valleys, or test of our faith? We can read the examples of men and women who walked by faith and trusted God in the Bible. We can also look around the church and see so many great examples of people who are still trusting God, proving we can make it.

Faith ranks at the top of God's requirements of man.

Hebrews 11:6 KJV,
"But without faith it is impossible to please him:

for he that cometh to God must believe that he is, and that he is a rewarder of them that diligently seek him."

The only way to God is through faith. First we must believe that there is a God. Then we must trust God with all of our heart. Then believe that He is the one that rewards all of us who sincerely seek after Him and His will.

God is a just God. He is the one that gives each of the faith that we need to live day by day in this sinful society. He is the one that give each of the faith that it takes to be saved, healed, and delivered and to overcome. He gives everyone the amount of faith they need.

Romans 12:3 KJV,
"For I say, through the grace given unto me, to every man that is among you, not to think of himself more highly than he ought to think; but to think soberly, according as God hath dealt to every man the measure of faith."

Now that God has given us the amount of faith that we need, it is our requirement to keep our faith activated. It is up to us to increase our faith, to keep it high and to use our faith.

Romans 10:17 KJV,
"So then faith cometh by hearing, and hearing by the word of God."

We can keep our faith high and activated by reading the Bible daily. By the study of the Word of God often. By attending church and hearing the Word preached under the anointing of the Holy Ghost.

People are always asking, *"What is faith?"*

Hebrews 11:1 KJV,
"Now faith is the substance of things hoped for, the evidence of things not seen."

Faith is ~ is the confident assurance that we have. It is the certainty we have, that what we are hoping for and trusting God for is going to soon be attained. We believe this so strongly, even though we see no sign of anything changing in our life or in our circumstances at this moment and time.

Faith is ~ is our determination to still trust God, to still believe in God when we cannot feel Him. When we are in a dark valley? When we are sick, diseased or afflicted? When we are at the very doors of death we can still trust the Lord?

Faith is ~ When the heat is on, our confusions are mounting higher and higher, we are in the most horrendous crises of our life, doubt and fear begin to set into our mindset and thinking, we become totally disillusioned, despair has us surrounded? We still trust our Lord.

Faith is ~ In the midst of our frustrations, fears and despairing of life. We know that our God is the One that created this entire universe, simply by speaking it into existence. We still know beyond a shadow of doubt that He controls all power. He can rescue us. He can heal us. He can deliver us. But for some unknown reason to us, He doesn't. We do not know His reasons of why? But in spite of it all we still trust Him.

Faith is ~ When you are in the heat of your trial and you feel all alone God seems to have forgotten you, Satan and all the evil spirits are laughing and mocking you? You look back at them and say, "I know my redeemer lives, and though He allows this to come my way, I want you to understand though He slay me I still trust Him."

Yes, saints of God, Christian friends. When it seems like God is not there. When it seems like He has forgotten us. When it seems like He does not see or hear us at all. You know those times in our life when God is simply not making any sense. We must keep on trusting Him. Keep on praising His name. We must keep on loving Him. We must keep on keeping on. We can make it, we can overcome, as long as we keep on trusting Him.

2 Kings 4:1-7 KJV,

"Now there cried a certain woman of the wives of the sons of the prophets unto Elisha, saying, Thy servant my husband is dead; and thou knowest that thy servant did fear the Lord: and the creditor is come to take unto him my two sons to be bondmen. And Elisha said unto her, What shall I do for thee? tell me, what hast thou in the house? And she said, Thine handmaid hath not anything in the house, save a pot of oil. Then he said, Go, borrow thee vessels abroad of all thy neighbours, even empty vessels; borrow not a few. And when thou art come in, thou shalt shut the door upon thee and upon thy sons, and shalt pour out into all those vessels, and thou shalt set aside that which is full. So she went from him, and shut the door upon her and upon her sons, who brought the vessels to her; and she poured out. And it came to pass, when the vessels were full, that she said unto her son, Bring me yet a vessel. And he said unto her, There is not a vessel more. And the oil stayed. Then she came and told the man of God. And he said, Go, sell the oil, and pay thy debt, and live thou and thy children of the rest."

Chapter Six

"What Do You Have In Your House?"

I as an individual struggled in my walk with God, before I learned how to lean on Him. I had so many insecurities and complexes to deal with. But God uses these weaknesses of my life to teach me how to trust Him and to see that His grace is sufficient even for me. I wish that I had the know how to take all these situations of my life and the lessons that God taught me, put them into a lesson form or book form to teach young people and new converts how to lean on God.

I have learned something in my few years of life. We can write books and teach principles that we have learned. But the substance of all this will never hit home until someone else is walking in this same type situation.

This story that I have used as the setting for this lesson, "The woman with the pot of oil," is a very simply story. But in this simple story we find some very great principles about faith and dependency on God.

Sufficient Grace when Your Life is in the Sewer

We as Christian people need to know where to go when we don't know what to do next. This little woman, was a single parent. She had no means to support herself and her sons. She seemingly had no food in her house. The creditor had come knocking at her door to collect the debts of her dead husband. She had no money and no means to pay this debt. The creditor was threatening to come and take her sons as his bond servants or slaves. This little woman was a widow in a very bad predicament. If she did not pay this debt soon, she was going to lose her children to the creditor.

The only thing this little woman seemed to have in her favor, she knew where to go and who to turn to in times like this. Only God could help her now. She went to the man of God, the prophet Elisha, with her plight.

Christian brothers and sisters, where we place our trust, where we place our hope, where we even place our expectations in times like this, will determine our answers. If we look to man's ways to supply our needs and solve our problems, we will end up in total disappointment. But on the other hand, if we will trust God, in faith believing, He will see us through.

As saints of God, we will fight many spiritual battles. Because of this, we must always know where to turn for help, strength and answers. God is our ever present help in our times of trouble. God is our source of strength in every situation. God has all the answers we need. We must bring Him our request and petitions. Give them all to Him and trust Him to work them all out.

> Philippians 4:6 New Living Translation ®, *"Don't worry about anything; instead, pray about everything. Tell God what you need, and thank him for all he has done."*

Worry is our biggest problem as Christians. We get some bad news we begin to wring our hands. We wrinkle our faces into the shape of sadness and depression. We cry all the time. Telling everyone else, "I just don't know what I am going to do?" We rehearse these complaints over and over. We complain, moan and groan to our self, until our nerves are shot. We tell everyone that we see about all of this bad news.

What have we accomplished? NOTHING! We have just caused our own nerves to be shot. We get no sleep, because we spend our nights in worry. We are causing our hair to turn gray. We are causing ourselves to have stomach ulcers. Our blood pressure is out of control, our heart rate cannot seem to be controlled. We are causing ourselves more doctor bills and medication bills.

I have realized over the past twenty or so years, we have had more Christians who have died trusting in doctors and the medical field than we have who have died trusting in God.

If we will just learn to give our problems and situations to the Lord, put our faith and trust in Him, stop moaning and crying all the time. Only mention it to God in prayer, continue to live for God. Our faith would begin to increase and we would begin to see greater results.

Notice the answer that Elisha gives this little widow woman. "What shall I do for thee?" In our words today, Elisha was asking her, "Well sister, what did you come to me for?"

My personal opinion is this: This great man of God, "Prophet of God," was refusing to let this little widow woman put her trust in him as a mere man. He was directing her faith and trust to God.

Unfortunately it is not that way in the Christian church world today. We are living in a celebrity oriented Christian society. If we just get prophet or prophetess so and so, they would be able to give us the answers we are searching for. Evangelist so and so is really working in the gifts today. Just get him here he will call them out read their mail and will solve all of our problems. We have so many faith healers who are going around and only they can heal the sick, without them praying the prayer of faith our sick will never be healed.

As saints of God today, let's stop being dependent upon men and let's go back to trusting Jesus Christ with our problems, petitions and situations. Jesus Christ is our only hope today.

I am not teaching in this manuscript, not to call your pastor and church for prayer. I am not saying do not go to your pastor for council when you have problems and trials. I am not even telling you not to call other saints of God to pray for you in these matters. It is biblical to call for prayer when you are sick, afflicted and in need.

James 5:14-15 KJV,
"Is any sick among you? let him call for the elders of the church; and let them pray over him, anointing him with oil in the name of the Lord: And the prayer of faith shall save the sick, and the Lord shall raise him up; and if he have committed sins, they shall be forgiven him."

What I am trying to get across to you is not to put you hope and trust in men, but put it in God. Like this needy little widow woman, we get so caught up in our troubles, and cares of life. That all we can see is the negatives, the doom, the gloom, and the despair. We simply see how little we have and we get caught up in looking at the things we do not have. We are then overlooking the possibilities in those things that we do have.

Elisha did not try to set this little widow woman's vision on her need. He knew she was well aware of what she was in need of. But he tried to redirect her thinking, to increase her faith. He simply ask, "What do you have in the house?" He was trying to get her mind off those things she did not have and get her to thinking what she did have.

If you and I can only see what we do have, even though it may be insignificant, little or small, we have the beginnings of our miracle or our blessing?

Our first reaction to any crises is always negative. "Nothing is right!" "Everything is wrong!" "I have no hope!" This is exactly the way the little widow woman started out, negative, pitiful, so destitute.

> 2 Kings 4:2 (b) KJV,
> *"...And she said, Thine handmaid hath not any thing in the house,"*

But she thought and quickly changed to the positive

> 2 kings 4:2 (end) KJV,
> *"...save a pot of oil."*

It is so very easy to say, "I have nothing," but it takes faith to say, "I have nothing save a pot of oil." Somewhere in that moment of doubt we have a thought in our mind that switches from the negative to the positive. I have one small, little, tiny asset. It is so insignificant, but I do have it. Because it is mine, I give it to God.

The reason that so many folks are not blest by God, is because they refuse to give Him what they have. They simply do not trust God with their insignificant, little bit.

When we give our little bit to God, it really does not matter how insignificant it is. God will bless it and multiply it. God will use that little bit that we give Him to bless us and to provide our miracle.

Faith, does not deny your present reality. Faith just acknowledges, that in spite of your present reality, anything is possible with God.

> Matthew 19:26 KJV,
> *"But Jesus beheld them, and said unto them, With men this is impossible; but with God all things are possible."*

Today there are so many Christian people who are deceived by false teachings that they have accepted as the teaching of Jesus. They are taught to make positive confession, saying, I have no troubles, I have no sickness, I have no disease. All the while their lives are full of problems. They are taught to testify of the miracle in their lives, even though it has no taken place yet. I say to this, "Hog Wash," this is pure deception and a lie to one's self and to others that hear. This is actually a testimony against God and is not an act of faith at all. We must be positive and upbeat, but the Lord does not need our charades to produce His powerful anointing.

Elisha did not tell this little widow woman to confess that she had no problems. She was not told by this great prophet of God to testify of her miracle in advance. Elisha just directed her to see the positives, which changed her thinking and strengthened her faith to overcome the negatives that were so prevalent in her life at the time. She saw what she called nothing turn into a tiny small something, that actually became the answer to produce her miracle.

We today must realize, FAITH is not really FAITH until we as individuals take action.

James 2:14 New Living Translation ®,
<u>Faith without Good Deeds Is Dead</u>
"What good is it, dear brothers and sisters, if you say you have faith but don't show it by your actions? Can that kind of faith save anyone?"

Elisha told the little widow woman to "GO." She had to take some personal action, she had to get involved, and she had to work to get herself out of this dire predicament she and her sons were in. She was told to go and borrow empty vessels from her neighbors to see the completion of her miracle and blessing.

For her to receive all that God had for her and her sons she had to get out of her own home, go to every neighbors home and borrow their empty vessels. She had to lay aside all pride and what some people would even class as her dignity. She had to tell her neighbors her situation. She had to convince them that she needed their empty vessels. I can only imagine some of the questions and ridicule that she faced among her neighbors. But for her to save her sons she had to get involved for this miracle to happen in her life.

Saints of God let us remember this:

Two thirds of the word "GOD" is "GO." One third of the word "GOSPEL" is "GO." Because of this I am convinced that both God and His Gospel are filled with action. For us to have faith in God, we must go. For us to be a participant in His Gospel we must Go. God and His gospel are words of action.

For us in this hour to receive our own blessings, our own miracles we must "GO." We must get our neighbors, friends and even our families involved. While we are being blest they too will receive a blessing.

The problem I see as a pastor, is to many saints of God are sitting back, waiting on God to work in their behalf. All the while they themselves refuse to take action on their own behalf. They are unwilling to step out and prove their faith in Him.

Saints of God, UNBELIEF is not expressed by what you do. UNBELIEF is expressed by what you refuse to do. "I refuse to make me altar and pray daily." You will not hear from God. "I refuse to go down during a church service and be anointed and prayed for." You will not be healed. "I refuse to get involved with anything at my church." Then God will not get involved with you. Where there is no action on the believer's part, there is no faith.

Hebrews 11:6 KJV,
"But without faith it is impossible to please him: for he that cometh to God must believe that he is, and that he is a rewarder of them that diligently seek him."

Every supernatural blessing comes from God. For them to come into fruition we as human beings have to take action and get involved. By taking action we are proving our faith in God. I have learned, if we do nothing, we receive nothing. Faith + nothing = faith, but faith + our actions = God's reaction. Our action is the attraction for God.

Faith is not the belief that God will do everything that we want. Faith is the belief that God will do what is right in our lives, in spite of what we want.

Does your faith move mountains or do the mountains move your faith?

We can never put limitations on God's ability to provide, deliver, heal, save or to perform miracles.

Genesis 18:14 (a) KJV,
"Is any thing too hard for the Lord?..."

Jesus answered, Matthew 19:26 (b) KJV,
"...but with God all things are possible."

2 Kings 4:3 KJV,
"Then he said, Go, borrow thee vessels abroad of all thy neighbours, even empty vessels; borrow not a few."

Elisha was basically telling this little widow woman, do not limit God. "GO," borrow every empty vessel you can find. God will fill every empty vessel you can get into your house.

So many of us tonight, put limits on God. Because of these limits we place on God, we do not see the great results that we could be seeing. First of all we are afraid to go out and get the empty vessels and bring them to the Lord. We feel if we tell someone God can heal them; God can fill the; or God can meet their needs. Then after we have gotten them to Him and it does not work the way we thought it should, then we are a failure.

No saints of God we have it all wrong. Our task is to get these empty vessels to Him. He is the Healer. He is the Deliverer. He is the Savior. Let's get theses empty vessels to Jesus and let Him do the work for them.

2 Kings 4:4 (a) KJV,
"And when thou art come in, thou shalt shut
the door upon thee and upon thy sons,..."

Elisha was telling her to shut the door on doubt, fear and all of the negatives that could nullify her miracle. Saints of God we need to shut the door on doubt, fear and these negatives also. There will always be naysayer's among us. These folks are the speakers of doom and gloom. They will say this has been tried before and has failed, it will not work. There will always be those who will ridicule you. Laugh at you. Mock you. Who will tell you, you are so foolish in trying to do this that you are doing.

Jesus cautioned, Mark 4:24 (a) KJV,
"And he said unto them, Take heed what ye hear:...."

Jesus knew that we human beings will always act or react to those things we hear, from those around us. The seed of doubt quickly grows and flourishes when we are down and out, or when we are in deep despair. It is then that some spiritual nut gives us a word of doom, gloom and no hope.

Saints of God it is time that we learn to shut out doubt and fear. Stop listening to all the negatives of other people. Do not hang around those that reek with negativity. I refuse to hang around with negative people, I am kind and sweet to them, but quickly I am gone from their presence. These are my just a minute people. They want to take my time I tell them just a minute and I go to someone more positive.

This little widow did exactly what Elisha told her.

2 Kings 4:5 KJV,
"So she went from him, and shut the door upon her and upon her sons, who brought the vessels to her; and she poured out."

Many of our blessing and miracles are aborted today, by some bitter, disillusioned, critical church member. It is time that we learn how to shut the door saints of God. Stop entertaining these old critical attitudes and spirits that show up at our church; shut the door on them, do not let them even have a peak at your miracle.

Saints of God we must respond for our miracles and blessings. Elisha told her what she must do.

2 Kings 4:4 (b) KJV,
"...and shalt pour out into all those vessels, and thou shalt set aside that which is full."

This little widow and her sons provided the effort. God provide the miracle. As they poured, the oil flowed, filling the empty vessels. As long as there was empty vessels, the oil flowed. When all the vessels were full the oil stopped flowing. and the oil stayed. I believe, if they could have found one more vessel the oil would have filled it.

Do you know why we have so few miracles or blessings among us today? It is because so many of us have stopped pouring. It is not because all of the vessels are full. It is not because God's anointing oil has stopped flowing. It is simply because we the saints of God are no longer pouring. As long as we respond for the miracles, as long as we do our part and simply pour, God provides the flow of His anointing oil.

We cannot get mystified by some blessings or miracles that happened in our past. We must have fresh blessings and miracles flowing in our midst today. Sadly today so many of us worship the miracles of our past and fail to worship the miracle worker and provider of today. It is no sin to testify about all God has done as far as miracles and blessings. It is not wrong to reminisce about the things God has done for us. But we must move beyond yesterday. There is so much that God wants to do now, today. There are so many blessings and miracles still to come.

God does not provide us with blessing and miracles, to entertain Christians, and to make us shout or worship louder. He provides us with blessing and miracles always for a divine purpose. There was a divine purpose in the miracle of this oil.

2 Kings 4:7 KJV,
"Then she came and told the man of God. And he said, Go, sell the oil, and pay thy debt, and live thou and thy children of the rest."

Sufficient Grace when Your Life is in the Sewer

The divine purpose was first to pay her husband's debt, and spare her two sons from slavery, secondly for her and her children to live off the rest.

Miracles and blessings are so far above human understanding. If we are not careful we get caught up in the great wonders of it all and miss the divine purpose that God has for us.

What do you have in your house at this moment? If you will give it to God and you will "GO" get involved. God will do the rest. Many folks will be touched, changed, healed, filled and delivered.

Daniel 3:19-21 KJV,
"Then was Nebuchadnezzar full of fury, and the form of his visage was changed against Shadrach, Meshach, and Abed-nego: therefore he spake, and commanded that they should heat the furnace one seven times more than it was wont to be heated. And he commanded the most mighty men that were in his army to bind Shadrach, Meshach, and Abed-nego, and to cast them into the burning fiery furnace. Then these men were bound in their coats, their hosen, and their hats, and their other garments, and were cast into the midst of the burning fiery furnace."

CHAPTER SEVEN

"When Your Faith Is Tried By Fire"

Shadrach, Meshach, and Abednego were Hebrew boys who were taken captive into Babylon. Their names had been changed by their captors. Their Hebrew names were, Hananiah, Mishael and Azariah.

The command had gone out to all the people of Babylon. They were brought before a golden image of king Nebuchadnezzar. There they were commanded to bow before the image. If they would not bow to the image they were to be thrown into a fiery furnace. This was a sentence of death by burning.

The reply of these three Hebrew boys was nothing less than classic:

> Daniel 3:16-18 KJV,
> *"Shadrach, Meshach, and Abed-nego, answered and said to the king, O Nebuchadnezzar, we are not careful to answer thee in this matter.*
> *If it be so, our God whom we serve is able to deliver us from the burning fiery furnace, and he will deliver us out of thine hand, O king.*
> *But if not, be it known unto thee, O king, that we will not serve thy gods, nor worship the golden image which thou hast set up."*

The faith of these three Hebrew boys was proven to be real that day. God, whom they served with all their heart, was able to deliver them, from the burning fiery furnace and from the hand of the king. But if He chooses not to, our mind is made up; we will not bend or bow. We will not be devastated, nor will we judge God foolishly. We simply will trust our God forever.

These three Hebrew boys, faith, was not geared to their circumstances. Their faith was firmly attached to God. In total disregard to their personal fate and outcome, God was the central focus of their faith. They were not even focused on their own deliverance.

Oh, that we the saints of God, of this modern era, could learn the principle of faith from these young heroes who were slaves in Babylon! The fact that God could deliver them was not a surprise to them. But neither did their faith demand that it happen.

Today we have so many Christian people who tie their faith to some supernatural happening. Because of this so many are sorely disappointed. When our faith demands certain supernatural results, we as saints will often become disillusioned, because our expectations are not met. This is why so many Christian people are shipwrecked today. Our faith cannot demand our faith must trust God no matter what happens to us.

We must learn to trust God as these three Hebrew boys trusted God. We must allow God to fulfill His will no matter what we encounter. Whatever the results, we must trust God and plan to always remain faithful to Him. If we are delivered through the trial, we must continue to praise God! If we are not delivered through the trial, we must continue to praise God!

Job 1:21 (b) KJV,
"...the Lord gave, and the Lord hath taken away; blessed be the name of the Lord."

When you and I say, *"God's will be done."* This is not to make God the guilty party or the instigator of the losses that we suffer. God is not the one that brings these bad things into our life. God wills us to be whole, but we are born into a sin filled world that brings bad things to the just and the unjust.

Our Christian churches teach and speak so many erroneous, false ideas and philosophies when people are facing tragedies, losses or even deaths. We have this overused false expression, *"we don't understand but, it must have been God's will."* I will say, "Hog Wash" to these false ideas that are so prevalent among the saints of God today. The New Testament scriptures never show's that death, disease, suffering, destruction or any other evil to be the will of God.

John 10:10 KJV,
"The thief cometh not, but for to steal, and to kill, and to destroy: I am come that they might have life, and that they might have it more abundantly."

Satan is the thief that has come to destroy mankind. He is the one that causes bad things to come even to the lives of saints of God. But Jesus emphatically told us He came that we might have life and that it might be more abundant.

1 John 3:8 (b) KJV,
"...For this purpose the Son of God was manifested, that he might destroy the works of the devil."

Luke 19:10 KJV,
"For the Son of man is come to seek and to save that which was lost."

It is the will of God for everyone to be saved, healed, delivered and filled with the Holy Ghost.

2 Peter 3:9 KJV,

"The Lord is not slack concerning his promise, as some men count slackness; but is longsuffering to us-ward, not willing that any should perish, but that all should come to repentance."

In spite of all that Jesus Christ has done to seek and to save mankind. In spite of the fact that He is not willing that any perish. Our temporal life remains temporary, it is short and full of trouble. As long as we are alive here, we will encounter natural disasters. We will have accidents to overcome. We will fight the organisms and germs that cause us to become sick, afflicted and diseased. These things that we face can be temporary setbacks in our body or they can lead to our death.

As long as we are in this fleshly body, we will be subject to the problems of the flesh. Our Lord Jesus Christ may deem it in the best interest of His will and purpose, to deliver us from some of the diseases, sicknesses and problems we face. But we must understand, there will come, to each of us that point in time either sickness; disease or accident will remove us from this life.

I am of the opinion that it is God's ultimate will for you and I, to go to heaven to be with Him. It will be in heaven that we will never again be subject to pain, suffering, heartache, strife nor death again. In heaven He will wipe all our tears away and we will rejoice in His presence for ever more.

According to the Bible, the faith of the three Hebrew boys was pure. Their faith got God's attention, while they were in the midst of their trial. God paid them a personal visit while they were in the fire of the furnace. Faith says, "God is good all the time, in all situations and His judgments are without fault."

This approach that Shadrach, Meshach and Abednego took would be so very profitable approach for each of us to take. If we took their approach more often, we would hear less false prophecies concerning healing, deliverance and even salvation. Remember the approach the three Hebrew Boys took.

Daniel 3:16 (b)-18 (a) KJV,
*"...O Nebuchadnezzar, we are not careful to answer thee in this matter.
If it be so, our God whom we serve is able to deliver us from the burning fiery furnace, and he will deliver us out of thine hand, O king.
But if not,"*

So many saints of God that I know and pastor take this same approach today. We must be very concerned today as saints, as a church, that we are not taken in by false prophets (preachers and saints.) We must take extra precautions not to be taken in by false prophecies, especially when it comes to healings and deliverances. These happening have become a big problem even in Pentecostal ranks today. There are many preachers and saint's who build their entire ministry, on what they define as "prophetic and gifts of the spirit." They say when they speak, it as though God is speaking direct through them. They say things they perceive about others, can be in the past, present or the future. They are also willing to be accurate about 60% to 80% of the time. They miss on 15% to 30% no one seems to be concerned. Of course we live in a world that is full of Psychic's, fortune-tellers, mediums and readers. These folks have a success rate of 10%, yet people still go to them and use them daily by the millions. Come on saints of God, we need to come out of that type thinking.

Deuteronomy 18:20-22 KJV,
"But the prophet, which shall presume to speak a word in my name, which I have not commanded him to speak, or that shall speak in the name of other gods, even that prophet shall die.
And if thou say in thine heart, How shall we know the word which the Lord hath not spoken?
When a prophet speaketh in the name of the Lord, if the thing follow not, nor come to pass, that is the thing which the Lord hath not spoken, but the prophet hath spoken it presumptuously: thou shalt not be afraid of him."

A prophecy focusing on healing and deliverance should be handled with much care. There are many people who are going to be touched by such words. We have many Christian people who think, that speaking out is declaring their faith. By speaking out in public they think, such a statement puts God on the spot and God will have to perform what has been spoken or declared.

I do not know why we as Pentecostals, allow such inaccurate teaching to flourish among us. Unfulfilled prophecies cause great consternation and confusion, for the families of the ill. Yet we still have people; even in the church that I pastor that will flock after this type ministry.

I was preaching in a small town. This small church had had a revival a few months before, with an evangelist who worked in "The Gifts of the Spirit." This guy called people out and read their mail every service. One night a young boy was brought in from another state. The boy was suffering with Leukemia the medical field was doing everything they could to cure him. This boy was so weak he was in a wheel chair. This preacher called him out began to prophesy over him, and praying for him. The preacher told the boy publicly that he would definitely receive his healing. He said it would not be instantly, the boy would have to go through much trauma and pain. He told the family the boy would actually get to the point of death, but in 60 days he would get out of that wheel chair very much alive.

The pastor came to my trailer drank coffee with me and told me the story. He said, He was really worried, because he had gotten a telephone call that morning. The boy was in the hospital and the family was called in the family was angry at God, and the church, because God was going back on His word. I told the pastor, God is not guilty. The evangelist and he as the pastor were guilty. The evangelist was guilty of being a false prophet and he the pastor was guilty for allowing such to take place in the church he pastored.

About 4:30 the next morning the pastor came to my trailer. The boy's dad had just called him from the hospital and chewed him out, told him, that he and the evangelist were false prophets. The members of his church that had brought the boy to the church to be prayed for also called the pastor and called Him a false prophet. Letting him know, they would not be back to church. The pastor was so very distraught, he did not know what to do or where to turn in his dilemma.

We Christian's should be careful today what we say and how we say it. We should be very careful to protect the faith of others, lest we let their faith be destroyed by extreme and unfounded claims or actions.

Today Christianity is so confused about the Gifts that Paul wrote about.

> 1 Corinthians 12:7-11 KJV,
> *"But the manifestation of the Spirit*
> *is given to every man to profit withal.*
> *For to one is given by the Spirit*
> *the word of wisdom; to another the*
> *word of knowledge by the same Spirit;*
> *To another faith by the same Spirit;*
> *to another the gifts of healing by the same Spirit;*

To another the working of miracles; to another prophecy; to another discerning of spirits; to another divers kinds of tongues; to another the interpretation of tongues: But all these worketh that one and the selfsame Spirit, dividing to every man severally as he will."

These Gifts are given by God to His Church. These gifts operate through men and women of the church. These gifts operate through saint's who avail themselves to the Spirit of God. These folks become the channel for God's supernatural expression. Saint's of God are used as the Spirit of God wills and directs.

These Gifts that Paul wrote about are not always resident in a particular person all the time. These gifts emanate from the Spirit of God, are demonstrated through people as the Spirit wills. Just because God uses a particular person over and over or more than once, does not mean that person possesses that certain gift; nor can that person operate as they will. It is very possible for an individual to avail themselves to God in a certain gift area. Then at the prompting of God's Spirit, thereby this individual gets used more often in that particular gift.

However, only God operates the gifts of the Spirit. The sovereign will of God is the single criterion for the use of the Gifts.

Our faith, our hands, our tongues and our obedience to God, become the instruments through which the Lord provides these phenomenal blessings.

In reading the book of Acts, a novice of the Word, might consider that mighty miracles, healings and wonders, flowed daily from every saint's hands; that great things were happening 24/7 from each of them. Careful study does not indicate that this was the way it happened. Miraculous events were happening, but not in every place at all times. The Apostles and early saints were not overcome with depression, at each sign of trouble, at the signs of reversals or sicknesses. When God healed them, when God brought them deliverance they rejoiced. But when God did not heal them, when God did not deliver them they still rejoiced.

> Philippians 4:4 KJV,
> *"Rejoice in the Lord alway: and again I say, Rejoice."*

They kept the Faith when all was well, and when it was not well. The peace of God ruled their hearts and minds.

Most that are reading this manuscript have heard messages about healings and deliverance in the New Testament. When we talk about healing in the New Testament, we talk about all of those who were instantly healed and instantly delivered. But for a moment I want to look at a few instances in the New Testament, where the folks were not immediately healed, even where they did not seem to ever be healed.

Epaphroditus of Philippi had contacted a serious disease while visiting Paul in Rome.

Philippians 2:27 New Living Translation ®,
"And he certainly was ill; in fact, he almost died. But God had mercy on him—and also on me, so that I would not have one sorrow after another."

The people in his home area had heard of his serious illness and his near death experience. For this reason I Paul was anxious to get him home, so they could see he did eventually receive his healing.
Timothy, Paul's son in the gospel seemed to have a stomach problem. This stomach problem seemed to be affecting his life.

I Timothy 5:23 KJV,
"Drink no longer water, but use a little wine for thy stomach's sake and thine often infirmities."

No doubt prayers for his healing had been prayed, but he had not improved. Paul was telling him how to help his condition medicinally.

Trophimus, a gentile saint from Ephesus, a traveling companion of Paul's was not healed instantly.

II Timothy 4:20 (b) KJV,
"...but Trophimus have I left at Miletum sick."

The **Apostle Paul**, himself suffered physical problems.

Galatians 4:13-14 New Living Translation ®,
*"Surely you remember that I was sick
when I first brought you the Good News.
But even though my condition tempted you to reject
me, you did not despise me or turn me away. No,
you took me in and cared for me as though I were
an angel from God or even Christ Jesus himself."*

We are not told what the Apostle Paul's physical problem was. Some commentators say he suffered from malaria, some say he suffered from eye disease. I personally believe he had a sight problem. Trying to figure out his affliction is not the big deal; the fact is he suffered for much of the time he ministered, never seemingly being healed.

2 Corinthians 12:5-10 KJV,
*"Of such an one will I glory: yet of myself
I will not glory, but in mine infirmities.
For though I would desire to glory, I shall not be a
fool; for I will say the truth: but now I forbear, lest
any man should think of me above that which he
seeth me to be, or that he heareth of me.
And lest I should be exalted above measure through
the abundance of the revelations, there was given
to me a thorn in the flesh, the messenger of Satan to
buffet me, lest I should be exalted above measure.
For this thing I besought the Lord thrice,
that it might depart from me.
And he said unto me, My grace is sufficient for thee:
for my strength is made perfect in weakness. Most*

gladly therefore will I rather glory in my infirmities, that the power of Christ may rest upon me. Therefore I take pleasure in infirmities, in reproaches, in necessities, in persecutions, in distresses for Christ's sake: for when I am weak, then am I strong."

The fact that I am trying to bring out; is this, not everyone that was prayed for by the early church was immediately healed. In fact, some like the great Apostle Paul lived life with many afflictions. I also notice these early saints did not fault the Apostles, or saints. They did not question their own faith; nor did they blame the Lord for their troubles or afflictions. In spite of their sicknesses and afflictions, they continued steadfastly in the faith; they continued as true believers regardless of their personal physical fate.

Saint of God, today, whatever our circumstances we should be faithful to God. We must rejoice with those who are healed by the power of God. We must rejoice with those who seemingly are sustained by God's sufficient grace. If God does not heal or even deliver us today, we know He will sustain us. We must understand both are proof of His might and power.

Paul's great affirmation of faith, Romans 14:8 KJV, *"For whether we live, we live unto the Lord; and whether we die, we die unto the Lord: whether we live therefore, or die, we are the Lord's."*

Job said it like this, Job 19:25-26 KJV,
"For I know that my redeemer liveth, and that he shall stand at the latter day upon the earth: And though after my skin worms destroy this body, yet in my flesh shall I see God:"

The Hebrew boys said it like this,
Daniel 3:17-18 (a) KJV,
"If it be so, our God whom we serve is able to deliver us from the burning fiery furnace, and he will deliver us out of thine hand, O king. But if not,"

You that are walking in the fire today, take heart. If God has not chosen to heal or deliver you, He will sustain you. This was proven through the faith; of the three Hebrew boys of the Old Testament; of the Apostle Paul and the saints of the early church. They proved God with a faith that did not focus on the miracle or deliverance itself; that did not mandate a miracle or deliverance. But their faith was focused on the Lord as the sole object.

Mark 11:22 (b) KJV, Jesus told His disciples,
"...Have faith in God."

Yes, faith in the fire still pleases God today.

CPSIA information can be obtained at www.ICGtesting.com
Printed in the USA
LVOW040751281011
252474LV00001B/1/P